SEA FISHING
FOR BEGINNERS

Sea Fishing for Beginners

Maurice Wiggin

DRAWINGS BY

W. J. Pezare

ADAM AND CHARLES BLACK · LONDON

First published 1970
New edition 1977

Adam and Charles Black
35 Bedford Row, London WC1R 4JH

©   Maurice Wiggin

ISBN 0 7136 1734 9

Printed in Great Britain by
WEATHERBY WOOLNOUGH, WELLINGBOROUGH, NORTHANTS.

CONTENTS

	LIST OF DRAWINGS	9
I	FIRST THINGS FIRST	11
II	THE TOOLS OF THE TRADE	18
III	THE G.P. AND THE SPECIALIST	59
IV	PIER AND JETTY FISHING	61
V	BOAT FISHING	78
VI	ROCK FISHING	94
VII	FISHING FROM THE SHORE	107
VIII	ESTUARY FISHING	121
IX	AFTERTHOUGHTS AND ALL THAT	135

LIST OF DRAWINGS

1. Conventional through-action beach caster 21
2. Reverse-taper or spring-butt beach caster 25
3. Multiplying reel on crank-handled rod 27
4. Typical fixed-spool reel 31
5. Traditional centre-pin reel 32
6. Diagramatic sequence of operations in casting with multiplier and beach rod **34-5**
7. Using a drop-net when pier fishing 40
8. Three boat rods with but a single butt . . . the interchangeable top joints are of differing weights and strengths 46
9. Double-handed (left) and single-handed (right) spinning rods 50
10. Close-face reel on cranked casting rod 52
11. Twin-hook paternoster tackle 64
12. Running leger rig 64
13. Knot for tying hook to trace 69
14. Ragworm on long-shanked hook 76
15. Lugworm on hook 81
16. (Left) Bar-spoon with feathers 84
17. (Right) Cutting a 'lask' of mackerel for hook bait 84
18. Roller rod-tip for heavy boat work 91
19. Bloodknot for joining lengths of line 99
20. Spinning flight for dead fish, such as sprats 101
21. Artificial spinner—the long narrow spoon 102
22. Typical conventional spoon 103
23. Light spoon 105
24. 'Jigger' lure 105
25. Baiting-up with squid 113
26. Rod rest 117
27. Tandem fly—Demon or Terror lure 122
28. Flounder spoon 125
29. Baiting with prawn 127
30. Heavy eccentric spoon 127

This book is dedicated to my cousin TOM BAXTER of Hanley Childe, a loyal friend even though he is more at home with specimen flowers than with specimen fish; and also to our mutual friend BOB KING, the phenomenal pharmaceutical phly phisher; and indeed to all that genial fellowship who foregather under the hospitable rooftree of the Royal Oak in Tenbury Wells, my home from home; and to MARGARET and TOM GREAVES who minister there, so devotedly, to the needs of the angler's body and spirit; yes, it is dedicated to all of these, and may the sun shine on my friends.

Chapter I

FIRST THINGS FIRST

Some little time ago, in 1953 to be precise, when the world was young, my friend and publisher John Baker asked me to write a little book called *Fishing For Beginners*. Which I duly did, to the best of my ability, and I'm glad to say it still sells briskly, in fact it sells more briskly than ever before. 'All things are relative', as the philosophical gentleman said, while slipping strychnine into his great-aunt Effie's nightcap, and the relative success of that little book has not enabled me to retire to a private beat on the Aberdeenshire Dee. However, it has kept me in cigarette papers, matches and pipe cleaners, and that's something.

Now the funny thing is that when John Baker commissioned me to write that book, it was taken for granted, by the author and the publisher *and* the public, that fishing meant freshwater fishing. What else was there? Of course we knew all about pier fishing, or thought we did, and we knew that hardy chaps sometimes went out to sea in boats and came back covered in salt spray and other things and incidentally toting strings of nice eatable fish. In fact I had myself been sea fishing, off and on but mainly off, ever since I was a skinny schoolboy prone to sea-sickness. I had a parsonical uncle—I had dozens of them, actually, but the one I mean lived in the manse at Portland Bill, a very fishy place—and here I learned from local professionals something of the hows and whys and wherefores of their trade. And I may say that is a very good way of learning, to go out with men whose actual livelihood depends on catching fish. Yes.

But later on in life I became a fervid freshwater fisher, first for the so-called coarse fish, later for trout and sea trout and salmon and grayling. I turned away from the sea to the inland waters for a variety of reasons which seemed good at the time. The chief amongst them was that in those days sea fishing was so crude and coarse that it did not really rank as a *sport*. The gear used was terribly rough and crude, and sea anglers frankly were despised, I mean by us finicky freshwater fishers, for their lack of subtlety. We saw no delicacy in their approach, and there was none to see. Frankly, we thought of them as little better than morons, lined up elbow-to-elbow along the pier at some ghastly seaside resort, dangling great lumps of lead on lines as stout as hawsers, using rods with all the suppleness of boathooks. That was the general impression we had. It was wrong, even then. But there was a germ of truth in it.

Now everything has changed. And I must confess that I am one of those who has helped to change the scene. Of course I'm not the only one, not by a long chalk. But best-selling little books like that little number of mine, plus the coming of a certain degree of affluence for the populace, and motor transport for more and more people—all this has meant that fishing has boomed in the most frap-jabberous manner. Fantastic. People with minds like computers and no morals at all have lodged a claim that three million people go fishing, making it easily the biggest participator sport. If you don't count swimming, perhaps. Well, I don't know how anybody works out a claim of that order, but neither do I care. Plainly there are a whole lot of fishermen around: you must have noticed. With the result that the angling waters of this blessed isle have become slightly congested. It is a sad fact that the availability of good fishing tends to decline as the number of people seeking it increase. Water abstraction, new building including road building, pollution, and popularity—all these factors work remorselessly against the freshwater fisherman. His opportunities tend to decline rather than to increase. Freshwater fishing is becoming a shade too crowded for some of us who like elbow-room and the sensation of being off in the wild places.

This is one of the factors, perhaps the chief one, which set slightly frustrated freshwater fishermen thinking about the sea. But there have been others. 'Coarse' fishing can still be had, very good coarse fishing, all things considered; but for some of us there comes a time when the business of catching a fish merely to put it back in the water begins to pall. Whereas game fishing—fishing for trout, sea trout, grayling and salmon—has become quite hard to find, and very expensive if good. I must say that to my mind game fishing, especially fly fishing, remains incomparably the most thrilling and satisfying aspect of angling; and this view is shared by many, too many. But it's a declining sport, on the whole: too many anglers chasing too few fish. And this is where the lure of sea fishing really comes in. It is, virtually, inexhaustible.

Inexhaustible from the viewpoint of the sportsman, that is. Some fishing grounds in the deeps have been fished out, one hears, and the battle of the trawlers has some frightening implications, I don't doubt. But it will take a hell of a lot of individual anglers to make much of a dent in the teeming population of the inshore waters.

And it is free. Free not only in the sense that no-one has to buy fishing rights in the sea, but free, too, of all the restrictions that hedge freshwater fishing around. The coast is free. The sea is free. If you can reach the water, you can fish it. You can fish it by night and by day. You can camp on the sea's margin and fish it round the clock without anybody's by-your-leave. You can light your bonfire on the beach and spend a thrilling night waiting for the pluck of the big cod, cooking bangers and bacon and brewing up hot drinks. You can roam the rocks and send your lure adventuring into the gurgling, pounding, sucking waves that swing the seaweed and the wrack in marvellous great whorls and vortices. You can go afloat and fish the tides around, no man's slave. You can fish every day of the year. There are no close seasons, no rod licences, no permits, no water bailiffs. The sea is free.

(I suppose that just for the pernickety but sacred purposes of accuracy I had better mention that at some points around the coast access to the water's edge is in private ownership and you *can't* just park yourself where you wish and start fishing. Of course this is the case. At such points the coast is not free. But, by and large, wherever you can *legally* reach it, the sea is free.)

And there are two more potent reasons for the increase in the popularity, and desirability, of sea fishing. One is the wonderful fact that much of what you catch is highly edible. There is nothing in the whole gamut of grub which tastes better than a sea fish cooked as soon as it is caught. Even a few hours later, after the journey home, it still tends to taste fresher than you would have believed possible. Of course there *are* some sea fish which don't rate high as items on the menu, but they are heavily outnumbered by the ones that do. I must say this means something to me. I don't mean that I'm always thinking of my belly, but as you grow older you derive less satisfaction from simply catching fish, inedible and useless fish, in fact you grow quite dubious about the ethics of that business. You want a respectable reason for indulging in your predatory sport, and the best of all reasons is that you are fishing for the pot. I'm not going wearisomely into the confused ethics of fishing now, but will simply say this, that if it comes to a choice between catching your own supper and buying it from a shop, the sportsman who kills his catch cleanly and instantly has no need whatever to feel ashamed.

Finally there is the technological revolution which has swept the fishing tackle industry in the last few years. Fishing remains, and will always remain, a basically simple pastime: but the tools of the trade have changed almost out of recognition in the late 'fifties and the 'sixties and the prime result is that sea angling is now a sport as seductive as freshwater fishing—more so, to some temperaments. The key to this desirable change is, in a word, plastics—actually fibreglass. The coming of fibreglass rods, nylon or terylene lines, and modern reels has meant a real transformation in the *feel* of sea fishing. Rods are not only much lighter in the hand, strength for strength, than they used to be, but the whole outfit tends now to be finer than it was in the days of the hickory barge-pole and the greenheart poker. Monofilament lines are much thinner, for their strength, than the old flax braids; much less visible in the water, too. Even the sturdiest rods, those used for pier fishing, beach casting, and boat fishing for big fish, are lighter by far than they were in my youth. And everything has been lightened, streamlined, and scaled down to match. This makes the handling of the gear much more of a pleasure.

Mark you, there remains, at all times, one limiting factor which prevents tackle being lightened and fined down so far as some of us would like. That factor is the sea itself. Not the sea fish—big though they may run, powerful though they may prove. No, but the suck and hammer and rip and race of the sea itself, the sweep of tides, the swing and pull of currents, the swirl of surf—and the ruggedness of the sea bed, crushing shingle, snaggy rock, tenacious weed—*these* are the limiting factors which prevent us from going so far as we might wish in the way of lightness. You can fish for mackerel with a trout rod and for mullet with a roach rod; for bass with a salmon rod and for flounders with a pike rod. Lovely sport it is, too. But for much of the time, you are controlled by the nature of the live sea itself, persuaded by its power into using gear a good bit stouter than your freshwater gear. However, it is *relatively* so much lighter and finer than it used to be, and sea fishing techniques have been so refined in the direction of true sport, that the advances made by industrial chemists and enlightened manufacturers can be used with a fresh pleasure, even by the man who is accustomed to gin-clear inland waters and the refined tackle and technique which such water calls for.

And this was certainly not true when Wiggin Minor, slowly turning as green as his grammar school cap, used to catch mackerel and wrasse, pollack and pouting and bream, with a handline, or occasionally with Uncle Sim's poker-stiff boat rod, near the upside-down battleship which blocks the South Entrance to Portland Harbour. I enjoyed it even then, I enjoy it far more now. Of how many pleasures can that be said, given the elapse of so many years . . .?

One last thing may be said in praise of sea angling. It is the healthiest occupation known to man. True, it may quite easily kill you. It kills several anglers every year. When we come to the appropriate moment, I will, as in duty bound, sound the alarm about boat fishing. I do a great deal of boat fishing myself, but never recommend anyone to venture out in a boat. Your safety in a boat is absolutely dependent on the skipper's knowledge, experience, and good sense. And even that may not save you. Boat fishing is heavenly, if you have the stomach for it, but it can be murderous. However, all forms of sea angling provide you with vast quantities of the best air available. Appetites grow out of all recognition. Sleep comes easy to the man who has spent a few hours sucking in the old ozone.

Nowadays, after fifty years of the game, I catch a few perch and pike, but otherwise leave the coarse fish in peace. I cast a fly and a spinner at appropriate times, for the beguiling trout and sea trout and grayling, the kingly salmon. And I won't pretend that there is any experience known to me, any physical or manual experience, that gives such a generous return, in terms of inner satisfaction, as casting a fly on the pearly surface of the stream 'where the bright waters meet'. Like poetry and poker, it is a human activity, a human invention, which provides the right person with uniquely exquisite thrills. But sea angling is altogether a more *robust* experience. It is ampler, more open-handed, more bracing and large-hearted. You are keenly aware of the elements in their more rugged dimension: the infinity of the sea, its relentless power and music, the vastness of it all—these factors brace the spirit. Or crush it. There is something in common between the sea coast and the mountain top: they can elevate and enlarge, just as they may intimidate, the human spirit.

A day's sea fishing may indeed be as tranquil as a day spent sitting on the verdurous banks of a disused canal. You may sit for hours on pier or jetty or harbour wall, dreaming away the sunshine in a placid reverie interrupted occasionally by inconsequent and indeed insignificant fish. But there are other occasions, the stuff of stories and dreams, which brace the whole system and infuse into the most torpid imagination those fleeting intimations of the heroic scale of life, which, once known, effectively banish boredom from the hours we have to spend in servitude between our acts of freedom and desire.

Chapter II

THE TOOLS OF THE TRADE

It is still entirely possible to catch sea fish using nothing more elaborate than a stout handline, wrapped around a wooden winder when not in use. Lots of people still do just that. But this book is really about the sport of angling, and angling—a word which undoubtedly comes from the angle formed by rod and line—really does mean fishing with a rod, and, preferably, a reel.

Despite all that I said in the preceding chapter, you don't actually have to buy a dizzy assortment of brand-new gear of the latest type. If your circumstances forbid extravagance, be sure that you can have a great deal of fun, and catch a lot of fish, with just one rod, one reel, one line, and a small assortment of hooks and traces and weights. Of course you can. I don't want to mislead you and I don't receive a penny commission from any manufacturer of fishing tackle. Alas. So although I am certainly going to give you some guidance about the best tackle for various forms of sea fishing, and although it is undoubtedly true that the appropriate tackle both enhances your chances of success *and* greatly increases your pleasure, you really must not worry if you have to manage with the minimum. You can still enjoy yourself.

Sea angling divides itself, not very neatly but quite understandably, into various branches; and for every branch of sea angling there is what you might call the optimum gear—the tackle best calculated to give you maximum sport and maximum joy. No one rod and reel is ideal for all branches: when you realise what the tackle has to do, and why, then you will understand why a certain sort of outfit suits one branch of sea fishing better than another—and why just one outfit will be ideal for only one branch and a compromise in all the others. So—

(1) Beach Casting

Beach casting or shore casting means that you are standing more or less at the water's edge and casting your bait or lure out into the sea. Now certain things follow from this, as sure as night follows day. One is that the fish you seek don't usually come right up on to dry land in search of food—often they stay well out, just beyond the breakers. So it follows that you may have to cast your bait out quite a distance, perhaps as much as 100 yards or even more. Now you cannot possibly do that using a stiff short rod. To make a job of it, you need a longish rod with plenty of spring.

Secondly, when you have got your bait out into the breakers or even just beyond them, it is going to take a terrific bashing from the water and from the sea bed. Even on a calm day, the action of surf is constant and powerful. The to-and-fro of the tide is relentless. You will appreciate that to *hold the bottom* your bait must be accompanied by a fairly hefty weight—a lump of lead which may weigh anything from two ounces to eight ounces or even more.

So it will be obvious to you that your beach casting outfit must be capable of throwing a fairly substantial weight a great distance. Therefore it must be not only springy, but strong: not only resilient, but powerful. These factors only come together in a rod that has been designed for the express purpose. It won't be a short rod. A short rod may be strong, or springy, but it can hardly be both. A longish rod, then, with plenty of spring and plenty of backbone.

This has all been quite well known for a longish time,

B*

but only recently has a really scientific intelligence been brought to bear on the details of design of such a rod. Not so very long ago the accepted beach casting rod was a pretty massive implement of ten feet long or a good deal more, tapered throughout fairly evenly. Since the tip has to be strong enough to bear the strain of hurling out up to a half-pound of lead, it follows that the butt, in a conventionally tapered rod, is pretty massive. Such a rod, when made of built-cane or greenheart, weighs rather a lot. That is a polite understatement: it weighs a darn sight too much. In fibreglass, it weighs much less but is still a fairly formidable tool and not quite so effective as it might be (fig. 1).

But there came upon the scene, not so long ago, the truly scientific intelligence in the shape of a friend of mine named Leslie Moncrieff. Mr Moncrieff is a member of a small band of wizards, who foregather in a sort of coven in Hertfordshire, where they have cooked up many profoundly brilliant ideas which have changed the face of fishing. Other members of the brotherhood are the great Richard Walker, leading angler of this or any century, a Cambridge graduate and practising engineer by profession, whose approach to fishing has been more radical, and more fruitful, than that of any man breathing. There is my old pal Fred Taylor, the only man I know still capable of providing hedgehog pie for supper. And there is the resourceful Fred Buller. What a team that is! All these chaps, and others of the brotherhood, have made signal contributions to the art and sport of angling: I am proud to be their friend. But it is Leslie Moncrieff, leading spirit in the Moncrieff Rod Development Company, who has turned his attention to the salt water, and he who has effected a single-handed revolution in beach casting.

This huge strong man first came into fame, or notoriety, at the famous cod ground of Dungeness, where his prowess

1. Conventional through-action beach caster.

in hurling a lure far out into the 'Dustbin', where cod congregate at that point where sand meets shingle, first irritated and then awed his fellow anglers, who were consistently falling short. Leslie did not owe his startling success entirely to his physique, formidable though that is. Using his brains, he had divined the secret of the reverse-taper or 'spring butt' casting rod which makes it easy.

In its perfection, this concept was embodied in the Hardy rod known for a time as the Longbow; the most beguiling beach caster I ever handled. But, of course, other manufacturers marketed their versions of the reverse-taper or spring-butt beach caster: it was one of those ideas which are equally difficult to keep dark or to protect by patent. Indeed, the idea had been used long before in salmon spinning rods, notably Milward's Spinversa: and I suppose it might not be too far-fetched to trace its ancestry back to the 'vibration' type of spliced green-heart salmon fly rod, beloved of antiquarians, which, once mastered, enables a fit man to throw the weight of a soaked sunk line through a highly improbable series of parabolic figures, using variations of the Spey cast in a manner which should interest a contortionist.

The taper from the tip of the rod reaches a maximum thickness around the reel seat, and thereafter a reverse taper sets in, so that the rod is actually thinner at the bottom of the butt than at the hand. It is Leslie's contention (and nowadays few will dispute it) that the spring-butt action thus built in helps greatly to overcome the tendency to 'snatch', which be-devils all beginners who try to cast a lure a long way. The whole action of this style of rod is smooth and sweeping; the acceleration of the lure is sweet and jerk-free, the reel spool begins to revolve without snatch, builds up to maximum speed as the lure flies out over the water, and is sweetly braked to a stop as it enters the water. Over-runs, and the dreadful tangle known as a bird's nest, are things of the past. Or very nearly: some people can make a mess of anything mechanical. But the combination of a spring-butt rod and the appropriate reel, weight and line really do make long-distance casting something like child's play.

When I wrote the first edition of this book, in 1970, the reverse-taper idea was catching on like a virus: as I revise this text, in 1976, a reaction seems to have set in, and although reverse-taper rods are still available, and still behave as beautifully as ever, opinion seems to have swung back, to some extent, in favour of various combinations of tapers which are all basically based on the stiff butt. A little later on in this chapter you will find my reflections on the Abu Atlantic Zoom, a rather remarkable compound-taper rod which, I fancy, was instrumental in triggering off the reaction against the reverse-taper rod. It is largely a matter of personal taste.

I quoted a number of prices in the first edition. Galloping inflation has made nonsense of them, and since inflation is still with us and very likely to stay, I am chary of updating them now. But I will give a few typical 1976 prices, if only to provide some social historian of the future who may find himself leafing through these pages with a wry laugh.

Hardy's still offer some superb and very expensive rods, up to £40 for their strongest Tourney Surfcaster, but show a trace of compassion by offering the Victor Surfcaster, designed to throw weights between 3 and 6 ounces, at a mere £28-odd. But such a firm as Milbro offer a wide range of beach casters at prices from about £21 upwards, including one with a spring steel butt, and a very nice reverse-taper job, the Cutlass, at under £24.

More important than price is the physical capacity of the rod—as related to your own physical capacity *and* your intentions. If you are big and strong, so may your rod be;

if not, don't overburden yourself or you will find casting a misery instead of a pleasure. The real key is this: what sort of weight are you likely to be casting? A mere couple of ounces, or half a pound of lead to 'hold bottom' in a raging surf? I'm a fairly fanatical light tackle enthusiast myself, but undoubtedly the most useful all-round implement is a rod which will easily throw weights in the 4-6 oz. range. The dedicated cod fisher who faces fierce winter surfs may have to use a pound of lead: he needs a real strong rod. Any rod bearing the name of Hugh Stoker is good.

Aside from Hardy and Milbro products, I have seen and used thoroughly satisfactory rods made by Sealey, Martin James, Modern Arms and Auger: all good old makers. And the East Anglian Rod Company produce some pretty inexpensive sea rods which may well attract the beginner. You need spend a lot of money only if you mean to fish a lot, when the corrosive effects of salt air and water plus the knocking about which tackle gets on the shore really do wreak havoc on gear that is not sturdily made and prudently 'proof-finished' against exposure. The actual action of an inexpensive rod may well be just as good as that of a costly tool, but it is inherently less likely to have been expensively proofed against corrosion. So the occasional angler who really takes care of his gear, cleaning the rings and smearing them with a light film of oil after every outing, may well manage with one of the cheaper offerings.

And let's face it—some marvellously successful fishermen use some dreadful old tackle! So don't be put off if you can't afford the best and latest. Nice tackle is nice to own and to use, but bear one thing in mind—in sea fishing, the reel is more important than the rod.

The ideal reel to match a proper beach casting rod is, I have little hesitation in affirming, the multiplier. There are alternatives, but the multiplier is the reel which the rod

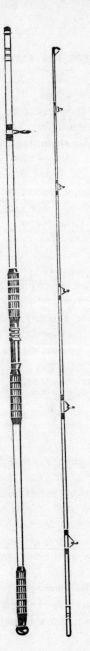

2. Reverse-taper or spring-butt beach caster.

maker had in mind, and although for some obscure reason
the very word frightens some people off, a few trial casts
with a friend's outfit will surely convince the Doubting
Thomas, that this reel is the goods (fig. 3).

What is a multiplier? As the name suggests, it is a reel
which produces several rotations of the spool for one
rotation of the winding handle. It is geared-up. Whereas
the simple old centre-pin reel gives you one turn of the
spool for one turn of the handle, the multiplier usually
gives you about three. But the intention is *not* a speedier
wind-in: the intention is subtler. The point with a multiplier is that the actual spool, on which the line is wound,
is of very small diameter, and very light in weight. When
this light spool is thrown free (by the touch of a lever)
it is capable of rotating very fast and easily. Even with a
light casting weight, it will turn at speed. With the gentlest
of swings, you can get your light lure moving out nicely,
sweetly. Whereas, a big centre-pin reel takes a deal of
mastering—the inertia of that big spool is formidable.
There is practically no inertia to overcome in the multiplier's light, small-diameter spool—the very minimum.
So little, in fact, that various cunning braking systems
have to be built in, including the centrifugal automatic
brake, which sounds a lot nastier than it is, in order to
prevent the spool from out-running the speed at which the
lure is travelling through the air, and thereby turning
the line in under itself and causing one of those bird's-nests.

But casting out is one thing, reeling in is another. Since
the spool is of so small a diameter, it follows that one turn
of it does not *put back* very much line: hence the multiplying gear, which gives you a quite reasonable though not
excessively fast winding-in or retrieving speed.

The multiplier was a British invention, but, like many
another, was greeted by our countrymen with nearly
unanimous lack of enthusiasm; with the result that it was

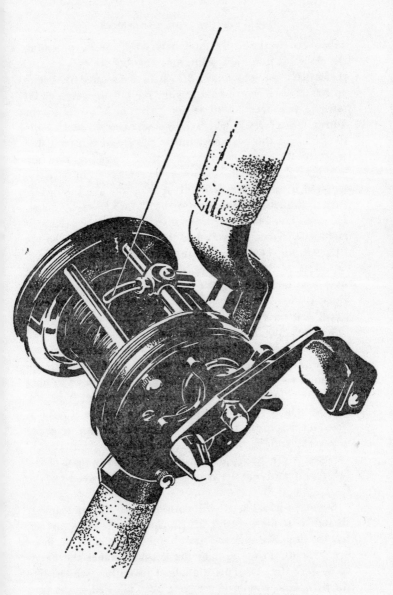

3. Multiplying reel on crank-handled rod.

taken up by dastardly foreigners who saw its potential, developed it to a high pitch, and now believe they created it. Latterly the odd sound British manufacturer has begun to make very decent multiplying reels: you won't go far wrong, or indeed at all wrong, with such a reel as the Intrepid Sea Streak, which is modestly priced, and ideally foolproof for the beginner. But it is still sad but true that most of the best come from abroad: topping the bill, perhaps, the beautiful Ambassadeur 6000 from Sweden, as good a reel as the Volvo is a car, and absolutely OK if you fish quite light—up to the 2-4 oz. weight range, I'd say. The Pfleuger (pronounced Flooger) Sea King is right at the top, a lovely handful of machinery. Like the Flooger, the Penn is an American multiplier. The Penn Squidder is their *pièce de résistance*; the angler's resistance may also be quite a piece when he learns its price. The Penn Surfmaster is as good as most of us want, or even need. A perfect outfit consists of the Ambassadeur 6000 for light work, the Penn Squidder for heavy work.

'Heavy' and 'light' are words which may need explaining somewhat. You are doing heavy work if you fish such strong or rough water that you need half a pound of lead to hold your bait in approximately the right place. You are fishing light if you can get away with a couple of ounces. The fact that in the first place you may catch fish weighing a pound, and in the second place fish weighing twenty pounds, is practically irrelevant. It isn't the weight of the fish that determines the gear you use: it is the weight of the lead.

Some people never will cotton on to the multiplier, though it is the sweetest instrument a man can play on, bar the liquorice stick and possibly the bassoon. Well, there are get-outs. Prime among the get-outs comes the fixed-spool reel (fig. 4). This diabolical invention, which, like the aeroplane, should never have been allowed, is the lazy man's answer to prayer. Since many of us are profoundly lazy, let's have a look at it.

It was invented by the ingenious Illingworth, in the 'Twenties, for the express and criminal purpose of casting a spinning lure of negligible weight (or even a worm) where a fly would have done just as well.

There is something divinely simple that marks this out as one of these great flashes of inspiration that come to peccable man every decade or so.

In essence, the fixed-spool reel is a reel in which the spool, on which the line is wound, is placed with its axis in line with the rod, instead of at right angles to the axis of the rod. Thus, if you were looking down the rod from the tip, you would see the lip of the spool broadside-on. When a retaining 'bale arm' is moved out of the way, there is nothing to stop the line from tumbling over the lip of the spool. Try it with a reel of cotton and you will see how it works. Perhaps it was watching a reel of cotton mis-behaving that gave Illingworth the idea. Anyway, that's the basic principle.

Of course the fixed-spool reel of today is a vastly more sophisticated implement than a cotton reel. With it, you can cast featherwieght lures a very long way, without the slightest effort. This is of course extremely flattering. Then when your lure hits the water, one half turn of the handle puts the bale arm back in position, and as you go on turning the handle, the line is laid more or less neatly in coils on the spool.

Most fixed-spool reels incorporate a slipping clutch, which you can adjust so that it slips just before the pull on the line equals the breaking strain of the line. Theoreti-cally, this means that you cannot be broken by the biggest fish, even with the most tenuous line. Theory is all very well, but you can break your own heart before you break the line, as well: standing there all night 'playing' a fish that deserves a quicker and cleaner fate.

However, grave as are the metaphysical objections to the fixed-spool reel, it is so easy and flattering to use, it makes the meanest of us feel a master, in a very short order. I confess that I have caught hundreds of fish on a fixed-spool reel. But ideally it should be reserved, in my view, for the casting of extremely light baits and spinners, too light to draw line off any other sort of reel. It has this place, and I must confess an honoured place, in the all-round angler's armoury. I should not personally fancy using it in sea fishing, except in certain special circumstances, but every man to his taste.

It certainly makes it dead easy to stand up there at the water's edge and within ten minutes have your lure flying out over the ocean—even though you have never before in all your life handled a fishing rod. It is the beginner's reel *par excellence*. I have to admit this. Why should I stand in your way, if you want the maximum ease of operation? Go ahead and enjoy yourself with a fixed-spool reel. It will make you feel a master. True, you will never get the distance which a *good* man with a multiplier gets; you won't enjoy playing your fish so much, for with all that right-angle bend of the line on to the spool, and that slipping clutch business, you will never *feel* the fish so intensely and accurately and personally as the other man will. But if this is the device which encourages you to start casting, so be it.

One thing in favour of the fixed-spool reel is that you don't need a specially designed casting rod to go with it. Almost any old rod will do. The spring of the rod, its graduated action, its suppleness and balance—these are all important factors when you are using other sorts of reel in which the spool revolves. But you can tie a fixed-spool reel to a broomstick and cast, after a fashion. It is the inherent action built into the reel itself which gets the lure

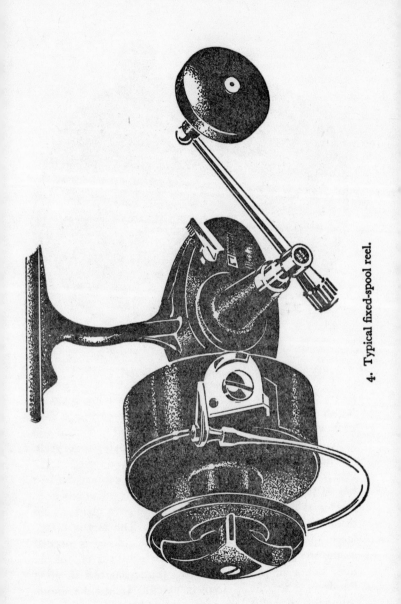

4. Typical fixed-spool reel.

31

5. Traditional centre-pin reel.

going out. True, a nice springy rod always helps, is always far nicer to handle: but, as I say, you can manage with rods which would not begin to give you satisfaction if you were using a multiplier or other sorts of moving-spool reels.

The traditional centre-pin reel (fig. 5) is still used on the beach, but few are the practitioners who can get the best out of it. It takes a good man, and a lot of practice, to master it. When I say master it, I mean get a good casting distance without dreadful bird's-nests. The inertia of the large spool being so high, considerable force is needed in the swing—and considerable weight on the end of the line. But a simple old-fashioned centre-pin reel in good hands is a wonderful implement still. It has the divine simplicity of really *basic* machinery, like a vintage Leica,

Rolleicord, or Model T Ford. A free-running Ariel fresh-water reel, such as used to be *de rigeur* for the salmon spinner, makes a good light sea reel—provided it is well looked after, cleaned every time, properly oiled. (I must say I wouldn't risk *my* old pal on the beach.) A rather more sophisticated centre-pin reel such as Hardy's Super Silex works well, too, but again it is a bit of a sin to expose such a reel to the corrosive effects of the seaside. Better by far to buy a reel made for the job, such as the sturdy Seajecta.

An audacious get-out, for people who like the effort-lessness of casting with a fixed-spool reel, but detest the mushy slushy lack of 'feel' when winding in or playing a fish, is the centre-pin reel that is so arranged that you can reverse the spool to make the cast, and restore it to its normal axis for winding-in. I think the first of these was the Jecta Orlando Supreme, which I think was devised, and certainly was manufactured, by another ingenious friend of mine named Gurney Grice. What I have done to deserve such friends?

Gurney saw as in a vision how to make the best of both worlds—something we all dearly like to do. Pressing a small spring, you whip the spool off the Orlando and pop it on a projection which sticks out underneath (what engineering language!) in the same axis as the rod. You make your effortless cast, take the spool off the lug and stick it back in its proper place, and wind in. Simple! Theoreti-cally you ruin your line in short order by building in wicked twist, if you don't remember to turn both sides of the spool to the front, on alternate casts . . .

A cunning method of overcoming difficulties is the Alvey 550 Sidecast reel. Instead of removing the spool and sticking it on that second axle, like the Orlando, you merely twist the reel through 45 degrees to make your 'fixed-spool' cast, and twist it back to start fishing.

Again, these ingenious reels may be used (though not

6. Diagrammatic sequence of operations . . .

to the best advantage) on virtually any old rod that is stout enough to stand the strain of casting whatever weight it is you have to cast.

You will undoubtedly suit yourself. And why not? And I shall undoubtedly go on proclaiming, in and out of season, irrespective of who's listening, that the ideal outfit for beach casting is a *fairly* long, specially designed, spring-butt rod, armed with a multiplying reel and the finest gauge line that conditions will allow.

I say *fairly* long, because I fancy that the craze for distance has resulted in some rods being longer than the average angler can really use to full advantage. We aren't all monsters (physically speaking, I hasten to say) like Leslie Moncrieff. Though actually his own rods are a moderate length, at 11 ft. 3 in. up. This seems about right to me: I am 5 ft. 11 in. and enfeebled by a long and perhaps not entirely healthy life among the ink pots.

... in casting with multiplier and beach rod.

Fig. 6 shows you the steps in a good cast, made with a proper rod and a multiplier. Having fitted up your rod, fixed the reel in its seat securely, and threaded the line through the rod rings, not missing any more than you can help, you then tie on the terminal tackle. This, which you will find described later on, when we actually get down to fishing, consists roughly of your weight, swivel or swivels, hook, and bait. (Don't worry about the details now: it all comes in its place.)

Now wind in until you have merely a few feet of line hanging from the rod tip—four feet is plenty, three will do. Stand with the feet a comfortable distance apart, at about right angles to the sea, with your left foot extended in the direction which your cast is to take. The left hand grips the butt at its lowest point, the right hand grips the reel seating, with the right thumb on the spool of the reel (assuming, of course, that you are a right-hander). Turn the body away from the sea and rest the weight on the ground behind you. When you are ready, with the thumb firmly on the spool, bring the body round strongly. Left hand pulls in on the butt, right hand pushes out. This puts a big bend in the rod. At the moment when the rod is about to straighten, in the direction of your cast, release the thumb pressure—but keep the thumb just kissing the spool while the weight flies out over the water. The thumb comes down firmly again as the weight hits the water.

There are of course many subtle variations on this basic cast. Some anglers lay back farther; some turn the body through a greater arc, some through a lesser. Some intrepid performers don't rest the weight on the ground but hang it from the rod tip, swinging it round in an aerial circle rather like an Olympic hammer thrower getting up speed. You will soon find which style suits you best. Whichever it is, it is the style for you.

The man from whom you buy your multiplier will explain, better than printed words can do, how you adjust the tension to suit the weight, so that the spool is just sufficiently free to make a good cast, neither holding you back nor egging you on to disaster. It's very simple.

I don't think I should leave this subject of beach casting rods and gear without mentioning the Abu Atlantic Zoom rods, which are conceived on a theory entirely at variance with the accepted canons of modern thought. The Swedish firm of Abu contend that the spring-butt is quite wrong: that casting power springs essentially from a stiff butt, and that the power stored into the butt by the angler's muscles, should then flow out through a resilient middle section and a sensitive tip. This is quite contrary to the reverse-taper thinking. Abu go further, and claim that by new construction methods progressive compound tapers can be built in which enable the rod to handle a remarkable range of weights. If you ask the rod to do little work, it does it efficiently, using only a fraction of its inbuilt power. If you ask it to do a lot of work, a lot more of the rod comes into play to cope with it. Thus the Abu Atlantic 484 Beachcaster is actually claimed to be equally at home casting a weight of two ounces or a weight of nine ounces.

Such versatility is pretty amazing. I personally enjoy the lazy swing of a really good spring-butt rod, but it is perfectly true that the snappier Atlantic Zoom rod really does flick a bait out in great style and with fantastically little effort. The much shorter handle and lower reel seating will also appeal to many who find their reach not quite wide enough for the usual wide spacing of hand-grips. There's no point in making yourself uncomfortable: quite the reverse. This is play, not work.

Though I love the lazier spring of the reverse-taper rod and have become quite at home with it, the more I see of the Atlantic Zoom in action the more I admire it and see its point. There is one other point, too: the spring butt rod is not so happy playing a heavy fish in strong water as is the stiff-butted Abu Zoom. This is a design which translates *your* energy—what you put into it—very precisely in terms of effective fish-quelling, as well as casting. It is up to every man to suit himself.

I said a little earlier that the Swedish Ambassadeur was as good as a reel as the Volvo was a car. I'm happy to say that when it comes to fixed-spool reels, the French Michell is as good a reel as the Renault is a car. It is pre-eminent among fixed-spool reels, in all sizes, and rightly so: it has earned its reputation. However, just as a British firm make, in the Intrepid, the easiest of all multipliers for a complete novice to master at one go, so the same firm in the Intrepid Surfcast come to the rescue of the patriot who doesn't want to spend more than he must. It is a very reliable reel at a modest price.

(2) *Pier and Jetty*

Pier and jetty are not identical, of course, but they share one cardinal characteristic in common. From harbour wall, jetty or seaside pier, you are likely to be dangling your lure and lead vertically down into the water—and hauling it vertically up. The architecture itself, pier or jetty, gives you your access to fairly deep water: you walk out over it. Thus, no casting problems arise, as they arise on the beach. You are not seeking distance—you've already got it. All you need to do (simplifying a bit) is to lower your stuff into the water, wait, and haul your fish up. (Yes, that's simplifying a bit.)

It follows that your tackle will be very substantially different from a beach caster's little load. No need for that superb casting rod—overhead casting is actually prohibited on a great many piers, and quite rightly, too. The danger to passers-by from enthusiastic casting could be quite considerable. But if your rod doesn't need the quite complex (and costly) characteristics of a casting rod, it does need something else—simple strength. According to the power of the tide that sweeps under the pier, you may need to use anything from a couple of ounces to half a pound of lead to keep your bait down on the sea bed.

It will be obvious that a slender, supple rod is out of place here. What you want is something burly, tough, masterful, with about as much give and play as a boat-hook. And that is more or less what you get in a pier rod. Well, perhaps I exaggerate: in fact I know I do. Some of the nicer pier rods do have an appreciable bit of life in them: but some are horrors. However, the ones that *do* have what you can honestly call a lively action, such as the Milbro Monarch, really can be used, quite well if not ideally, for other forms of fishing such as rock fishing and even beach casting. This is a tremendous factor for the man who can only afford one rod but who wants to get around a bit and vary his practice, as he assuredly should, if he is to get the most out of his hobby.

The pier rod is usually from about eight feet to ten feet in length. There are still some good built-cane jobs, but glass is winning all along the line. Hollow fibre glass makes the most responsive rods, but in these shorter lengths there is a lot to be said for the solid glass rod, which is cheaper. The Sealey White Wonder is a perfectly typical example of the most popular sort. I should add that some enterprising manufacturers have thought of the agreeable proposition of making a combination rod which will double for two branches of the sport. Such a one is the Auger Sea Switch, which breaks down into a 9 ft. pier rod or a 6 ft. 6 in. boat rod. Some makers, also, have heard of the cult of the drop net, and produce rods to match. This makes a lot of sense and might, in a way, introduce a touch of revolution into pier fishing, making it much more attractive to chaps like me who don't much fancy using boat hooks to catch little dabs.

The drop net, as you can imagine, is a bucket of net (its shape is really unimportant) held open at the top by an iron frame, and suspended by rope which is tied to a metal bridle (fig. 7). Having hooked your fish, all that way down in the sea, you lower the drop net—or, better by far, get a mate or curious onlooker to lower it for you—if you fancy the look of him—and when the net is sunk a bit, play your fish over it, and haul away. By this crafty method you are enabled to use a rod considerably lighter than the pole that is needed to lift a fish, dead weight, up many feet vertically. True, you still have to have a rod that will throw out the amount of weight needed to 'hold bottom' in the water swirling around the piers. But you can always throw it out by hand—it is always a mistake to fish too far out from the piers, anyway, since that is where fish congregate to get at the food hidden in the growth on the

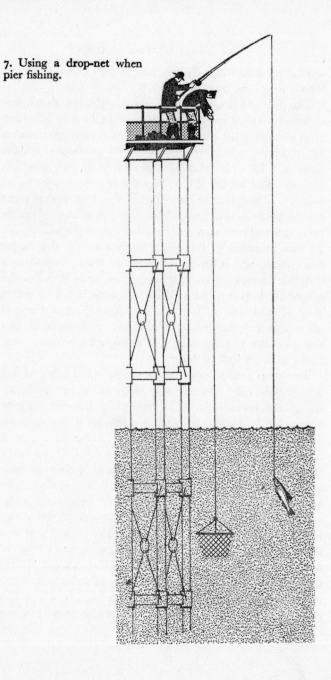

7. Using a drop-net when pier fishing.

piers—and other, better fish, come to get at *them*. With this in mind, the firm of Martin James market their lightweight Exeter-de-Luxe, an 8 ft. rod which will handle a casting weight of 2-3 oz.

The pier fisher's reel need be no more than a simple, rugged centre-pin job, the most old-fashioned reel in the world, such as the East Coast fishermen swore by, over the generations. A big star-back reel of walnut, now outmoded, is still just about perfect for the job. The Seajecta is the modern version in metal. This is really all that is needed —a gentle swing outwards to get your weight over the rail, and let it go down. But anglers won't be convinced that they might just as well fish under their feet—might *better* fish under their feet. So they go on making prodigious efforts at casting, with rods unsuited for distance casting. Good luck! I like to see chaps enjoying themselves. The multiplier, again, is quite in order on the pier. I see fixed-spool reels in use, all over the place, but there was never a less congenial use for them.

(3) *Rock Fishing*

Rock fishing is perfectly fascinating, lonely, arduous, sometimes a little dangerous, productive, exhausting, and highly educative. If you live long enough to assimilate what you learn.

The rock fisher catches several species but his principal quarry is bass, as they come nosing in with the tide. The rock fisher's sport most nearly approximates—though it still isn't all that near—to the freshwater fisher's. He is on dry land, or land that is approximately dry, and he is more flicking than casting his lure into relatively deep, or deepish, water, very near to hand. He is not using heavy weights, he is not holding his lure on the bottom in a great surge of surf, he is not venturing down vertically into immensely deep water like a boat fisher. What follows from all this? Why, it surely follows that the rock fisher's tackle comes as near as anything in sea fishing to the tackle used by the game fisherman inland.

There is just about nothing I enjoy more than rock fishing, in the heavenly indented littoral of the West. I am getting a bit rheumaticky for it now, more's the pity, but the West coast still calls strongly, the broken and embayed wild coast of Wales and the West Country (not to mention Holy Oireland) where you can range all day over tide-wet slippery rocks, dashed with foam, fishing for the gallant-hearted bass (among other fish). And until recently every hour of my rock fishing had been done with one of two rods—either a ten-foot sea trout fly rod, or a ten-foot salmon spinning rod. Every hour and every minute of it. Of course I don't say that you have to follow this example. By no means. But a light, single-handed rod that reaches out a bit, certainly not less than 9 ft. long, preferably 10 ft., eleven or twelve if you feel up to it—light, supple, strong and springy, a sport fisher's rod: that's the ticket.

One great day I rose before dawn in my little cottage under the Downs. I'll just tell you this tale while it's in my mind—put in my mind by this recollection of rock fishing with that game rod. We can spare a minute from being down-to-earth and serious, can't we? Right. I rose at the first tinkle of the alarm clock—odd how one who is a notably reluctant riser in the normal way can be out of bed, moving well, albeit like a sleep-walker, almost before the alarm clock starts to ring, when there's fishing afoot. I padded down to the cosy kitchen and brewed tea and fried bacon, fed the cats, packed away sturdy bacon sandwiches and a flask or two, and was on the road before sunrise. What a day that was to be.

I wasn't exactly doing it for a gamble, I was doing it for a story, being a journalist then as now. Much the same thing!

I headed West with the sun coming up behind me, the willing sun of May; I headed for the land of trout and sea trout and bass. And by the time the sun rose again I I had accomplished the following:

In the morning I fished for rainbow trout in a newly-opened municipal reservoir near Yeovil, and landed three over two pounds, all on a Teal-and-Red.

In the afternoon I fished for brown trout in the great lake of Chew Magna, and got one over two pounds, on a tiny nymph.

I drove on West, and in the evening, no, really in the first dark of the night, fishing a friend's water on the Torridge in Devonshire, I fished a team of Black Spider and Butcher for sea trout, wading in a fast stickle; and landed a fish that also just touched two pounds.

After appropriate conviviality at my friend's house, and the scant minimum of rest, as the sun rose again I fished for bass in the salt water of the estuary with a silver fly-spoon and landed one, exactly two pounds.

Four locations, widely spaced; four species, akin in their gameness; four lures, all different; four species landed, all just on or over the two-pound mark.

And every single cast made with that old sea trout rod. For it was the only rod I carried, though I had four reels and lines in my bag.

Pardon, your honour, I digress. The terrible gift of digression came upon me and I could not withstand it. It will happen again.

What is life if we cannot digress? The act of fishing is a continual or almost continual concentration—that is why it clears the mind so wonderfully of all the canting dross and knavery and junk of our daily worrying lives. But when we are talking about fishing, which is a different thing from doing it, why, then we may digress, it is our dignity and entitlement.

As I say, it may happen again.

But to get back to our slippery station on the wrack-wreathed rocks, the foam-spattered and spume-blown and weed-infested and tide-resisting rocks . . . All you need is a longish rod with plenty of give but also plenty of character, to let your lure slip out into the water almost at your feet. You may be float fishing, you may be lowering your weighted bait almost vertically, and silently, into the comparative depths, you may even be drifting it a little in the pull of the water, you may be jigging a lure up and down, which is marvellously effective on its day, or you may actually be spinning: but one thing you will *not* be doing, and that is hurling your lure out some prodigious distance. No, indeed. So you may leave that fixed-spool reel at home. Just as distance casting is self-defeating from jetty and pier, so it is self-defeating from the rocks. The prime reason why you are on the rocks is because the fish you seek come venturing right in to the rocks in search of their prey. If you cast well out, you are missing them. You just want something that will hold your lure out over the side of the rock, and gently lower it down. And the best reel you can use for the job is a simple old centre-pin.

(4) Boat Fishing

Men who stay ashore have no option but to wait for the fish to come to them. Sometimes, like the beach casting fellowship, they reach out into the sea, stretching out as far as they can to make contact. The big difference with boat fishing is that you go out to where the fish are. You seek them in the deeps, yea, verily, in the deep asphyxiating waters. Mind you don't join them.

Now one thing stands out solidly and that is that the man in a boat on the ocean has no need to *cast*. He has already arrived (or he *hopes* he has) over the shoals of fish. Ha! Yes. So all he has to do—and this holds true whatever method of angling he follows, whatever species he pursues—all he has to do is lower his lure into the water. He may let it go down almost vertically to or towards the bottom, he may let it stream out with the tide, float fishing or drift-lining. But unless he is actually spinning or fly fishing—they are the sole exceptions, and baby ain't they just exceptional? —he has no need to make a cast. Ergo, or as the multi-lingual would say, *therefore*, he stands in no need of a casting rod. Or reel. All he needs is a short rod capable of dealing with the weights he has to use and the fish he hopes to catch.

A *short* rod, brethren, because boat fishing, which is dangerous in every possible way, is especially dangerous when chaps start flailing away with their long rods. There are other reasons besides this excellent civilised reason, but it is reason enough. All you need, really, is a hand-line —you can fish very effectively from a boat with a hand line. However, you won't be *angling*. But a rod of five, six, seven feet long, as cheap as you like—a solid glass rod will serve splendidly—is all you really and truly need.

But of course there are boat rods and boat rods (wouldn't there just be?). Again, it is the work to be done that determines the power and weight of the rod. If you are fishing for massive great skate or tope or shark, you certainly need a doughty tool. But if you are just fishing for mackerel, you need nothing at all stronger than a nice trout spinning rod.

Again, there is a distinction that has nothing to do with the quarry you seek. Are you fishing a lure on the bottom of the sea, in a heavy tide rip? In that case you may actually need *several pounds* of lead to 'hold bottom' (and sometimes even several pounds won't do the job). Very often, you'll need as much as a pound of lead; quite normally, half a pound. These are severe weights for a rod to take, weighed

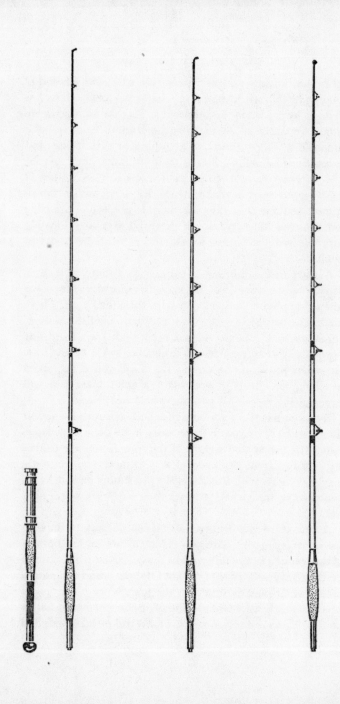

as dead weight (the rod never feels the weight of a fish as dead weight—or shouldn't). So often you need a stocky, chunky rod, even though the fish you seek may be quite smallish. But again, you may be float fishing, or drift-lining—streaming the lure away in the current of the tide, fishing it quite near the surface. In that case you need little or no weight, and a light supple rod will serve you quite well. Or of course you may be actually spinning, in which case your spinning rod *is* your boat rod.

Moncrieff and Hardy came together in offering a boat rod consisting of one butt with three tops of varying strengths, thus giving you a comprehensive outfit for the price of a comprehensive outfit . . . what could be more practical? The name Sidewinder has vanished from their catalogue, but the idea lives on. The *anodised* Longstone reel with Bickerdyke line guard comes into its own here.

Other makers may well follow this crafty idea. But in the meantime, while a-waiting (for Ernie or Littlewoods or the coming of heaven on earth) you may have to make do with one inexpensive boat rod. In that case you should treat yourself to a nice six or at most seven foot glass rod, hollow or solid but preferably hollow if you can raise the wind, and capable of handling a 'casting' weight of about twelve ounces. Such rods, more or less, are the Milbro Mermaid, the Abu Pacific, the very economical Sportex 3206, the Martin James Conger, or the Modern Arms Dover. And there are others: Rudge make good cheap rods. All fine rods, all reasonably priced (though the Abu, a very fine rod, is rather dearer than some) and all wholly at your service. The Sealey 'Hugh Stoker' which also gives you a choice of tips that fit one butt joint is excellent.

---

8. (*Opposite*) Three boat rods with but a single butt . . . the inter-changeable top joints are of differing weights and strengths.

Don't take your fixed-spool reel aboard, if you can help it. You want a solid old-fashioned centre-pin, for preference, or, if you like, a rugged multiplier with lots of line capacity.

(5) *Spinning*

You know what spinning is? Spinning means this: you cast out a lure which spins, or merely flutters and throbs and flaps around in the water; and having cast it out you proceed to reel it back in. While it is in the water it is behaving like a living organism—usually a small fish, and oftener than not, an injured small fish. It is your hope, and occasionally your belief, that the spectacle of this small party trying desperately to escape will arouse the unfriendly attention of some merciless predatory fish, preferably large. If such a predator makes a grab at your lure, he discovers, too late, that it is furnished with a hook, if not hooks. That is the essence of what is loosely called spinning. As I said, some so-called spinners don't spin at all, but they all make some sort of irregular movement in the water. Sometimes you mount a dead small fish, a prawn or sandeel, on a spinning flight equipped with vanes that make it spin in the water, and cast it out in the same way. Most times you use an artificial. Anyway, you are spinning.

Now a spinning rod is quite specialised and you cannot really go spinning without one. You cannot cast a light lure (and most spinning lures are very light) with a powerful stiff poker of a rod. You cannot really cast a spinning lure with anything *but* a spinning rod. Like a fly rod, it is a specialist tool which has built into it the necessary characteristics. With a spinning rod and the appropriate reel you will assuredly find it so easy, and so enjoyable, to *flick* your light lure out, over considerable distances, that you may come to rate spinning extremely high in the long catalogue of angling's joys. I do so myself.

Spinning is something quite new to most sea fishers, though it has been standard practice for the game fisher and pike fisher on inland waters for a very long time. But now that fibreglass and its allies have made it more practicable, sea spinning is catching on, and I don't wonder, I don't wonder at all, for at one stroke it sets you free of the mess of natural baits (which aren't always there when you want them) and it is altogether an enterprising, artistic and productive method, the most spirited and sporting way of taking fish worth taking. Certainly you may use your freshwater spinning gear for sea spinning, if you like. But do remember to wash both rod and reel thoroughly in fresh water when you get home, and then wipe them over with the proverbial oily rag. If you don't, they won't last five minutes, as the saying goes. They really won't. Salt water is very corrosive. So be careful. Especially of the reel.

But any spinning outfit is right for spinning, and if you own one already you *can* make do with it, provided you really and truly look after it and lubricate it.

Spinning rods made specially for sea spinning are very nice tools in the hand. Almost invariably the rod is made of fibreglass, of course. The reel fittings and rod rings are (or are supposed to be) pretty well resistant to corrosion. (Not that that stops me washing mine in fresh water after every outing—nothing like being sure.) For mackerel, and their brethren the garfish, which have green bones but still eat well, a trout size fixed-spool outfit is perfect. For the sturdier pollack and bass, a pike or salmon size outfit is the thing. You can buy this outfit very economically.

I happen to own and use one of the loveliest spinning outfits made for the job, the Milbro Mariner, which is a 9 ft. 6 in. two-piece, double-handed rod of modest weight and magnificent performance, and with it I use the Ambassadeur 6000 multiplier. This is the sort of rod which

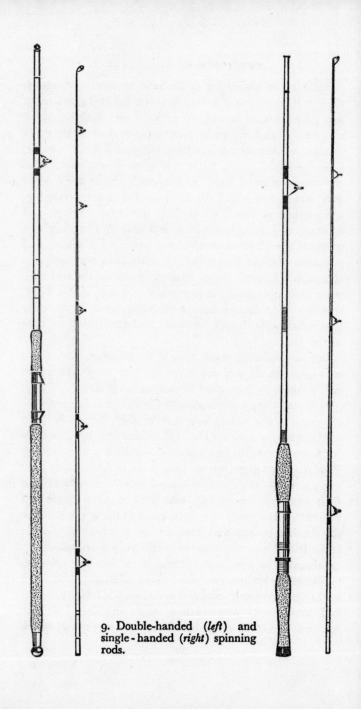

9. Double-handed (*left*) and single-handed (*right*) spinning rods.

gives you a fine feeling of *command*—in almost any circumstances, you can really reach out and get your lure where you want it. But there are many fine outfits to choose from —a rod like the 'Hugh Stoker' bass rod together with a decent fixed-spool reel will give you good command and line control.

For estuarial work, for rock fishing where a spinner is used, for harbour fishing, I like the longer rod, over eight feet and up to ten. But for many spinning situations and especially for boat work, a much shorter rod is quite handy, and will do all that is asked of it. In fact the nice little cranked rods, or perhaps I should say crank-handled rods, though barely five feet long, are really very seductive and beguiling tools for use in a boat.

A very nice reel to use with a crank-handled short rod is the closed-face reel, which is becoming more and more popular. You will see one illustrated. These closed-face reels are actually a variant of the fixed-spool reel, in fact they *are* fixed-spool reels, but all the fairly complex and vulnerable bale-arm mechanism is shrouded out of sight, in fact dispensed with, and as you will see from the drawing, the line issues out of a nice little hole in the middle of the front dome, without any bale arm flying around. This is perhaps the easiest reel in the world to learn to cast with —it does *all* the work.

You make your back swing holding a trigger down, and when the lure comes forward and you are ready to release it you simply take the thumb pressure off the trigger and out she flies. When it hits the water you simply start reeling in. It is all nice and compact and apparently guarded against the weather, though in fact you still need to look after it and clean and oil it when you get home. But this is an agreeable and attractive job, especially for people who hate machinery and want everything simple.

You can also use a small multiplier—in fact the cranked

51

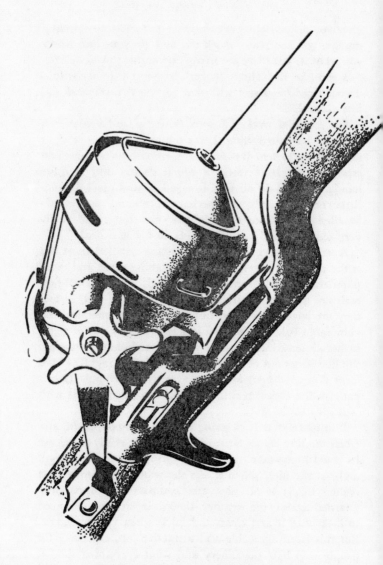

10. Close-face reel on cranked casting rod

rod was actually invented, or developed, in the first place, for use with a multiplier. It is a singular form of the truly single-handed rod, and heaven to use if you happen to like it. I once picked one up highly secondhand hand, from a junk shop, which appeared to be made of solid spring steel, in a hexagonal section. Many the good bass that fell to it. Cranked short rods are made in steel tube, built cane, solid glass and hollow glass. By their very brevity they assist the aim—they are aiming rods *par excellence*, and when using one you really do feel it is an extension of your arm (which it is) and it has some affinities with dart throwing and with archery. However, its aiming accuracy, which is unsurpassed, is countered by its relative inefficiency as a tool with which to play a big fish, once hooked. It provides the minimum of leverage and lift, and is the nearest thing to handlining. Each to his taste. It is a great little weapon in the boat fisher's armoury, for sure.

This has been a rather formidably long section on tackle. But you should know what's what, what is available and how it helps. I repeat that you can fish perfectly happily, and reasonably effectively, with whatever rod you happen to own, and whatever reel, too. But having one rod only will naturally cut down the range and scope of your activities.

When making up your mind what to buy, you should be guided by the facilities available to you. Are you going to do most if not all your fishing from a pier? From the beach? From a boat? From the rocks? Are you one who will spend his fishing time along an estuary? This is the important thing to know. If the great majority of your fishing hours will be spent in any one of these activities, then you can select the appropriate outfit and manage happily all your days with it. Don't you worry. You don't *have* to have a whacking great armoury of gear, lovely though it is to see ranged around the walls. But if you travel a lot, and adventure this mode and that of sea fishing, you *do* need something of a choice of rods and reels.

As I have said before, if you are already a freshwater angler you may already own an outfit which will serve you at sea—though it will almost certainly take a terrible beating from the corrosive effects of salt air and water, unless you treat it like the Crown Jewels. But a good pike rod will stand you in good stead, so will a salmon spinning rod; even a trout rod will come in handy for mackerel fishing; even a roach road will serve for mullet fishing.

One rod I haven't yet mentioned which is really wonderful for some aspects of sea angling is that excellent modern phenomenon, the carp rod. Our old friend Dick Walker practically invented this tool—the stepped-taper Richard Walker Mark IV carp rod set new standards, opened new vistas. Now rods based on that famous model, and made in fibreglass as well as cane, are quite commonplace: most of them being 10 ft. long and coming in two pieces. Such a rod is simply grand for a great many sorts of sea fishing, as you will see when you read on. It will even spin a lightish lure, up to an ounce or an ounce and a half, very adequately. It is ideal for float fishing and for drift lining and I've even used it for beach fishing. Of course it's not the job at all for hurling heavy weights, for boat or pier fishing. But it is simply perfect for rock fishing, perfect. This is the ideal versatility weapon for the sea angler who (like me) loves fishing light—really sporting, enjoyable fishing full of *feel* and responsiveness. There are things it won't do, but there are more things it will do. It is a lovely instrument.

Of lines, I will just say this. Monofilament nylon is now the most popular line by a mile, and rightly so. It is cheap, supple, strong and not very visible in the water.

It has quite superseded the old flax and cotton braided lines. But it does deteriorate, and since it is so cheap, it pays to break off the seaward end and replace it with new, quite regularly and always after a particularly severe battle, either with the surf or with a heavy fish. *Please* burn it, don't just throw it away. Abandoned monofilament can cause terrible suffering to birds, who are often condemned to a lingering death by starvation when they get themselves tangled up in abandoned lengths of line.

I will indicate appropriate breaking strengths in the sections on various sorts of fish and fishing. Many sea anglers seem to use line that is heavier than they need. They lose a lot of sport and fun by this. Remember, it isn't the fish, it's the surf, the rocks, the pebbles, the weed —the sheer weight and welter of water and detritus, that does the damage. If you're bottom fishing, you simply have to put up with it, using heavy weights and line. But if you're surface fishing, or more or less surface fishing —float fishing, drift lining, spinning, fishing the feathers or the 'fly'—then use a strength of line that is truly appropriate *to the quarry*. You'll have far more fun, more genuine sport. When fishing for mackerel with the fly or light spinner, I sometimes use a line of 2 lb. breaking strain. Why not? Mackerel won't break it, in the open water in which one pursues them.

There is another sort of modern line which instead of being one single extruded filament—monofilament—is of braided or woven filaments. Naturally enough, it is known as braided line—some anglers simply refer to it as braid, for their sins. I personally am very fond of braided terylene line—it is pre-shrunk, and supple, and lies down on the reel spool perfectly, whereas *some* monofilament lines, in the stronger gauges, tend to be a bit springy, and to ride up on the spool. I prefer braided terylene on a multiplier. It is far more expensive, though.

Pretty new is an American development which has a very bright future—a braided line made of polyester fibres, smooth and strong. It casts very nicely. It has the further advantage of being free from the stretch of monofilament. New monofilament stretches a lot—which militates against hooking your fish. If your bait is a long way away when the fish takes it, you have to heave pretty hard and reel in too, to overcome the stretch and set the hooks. Many good fish are lost this way. (And a complementary factor is that when you have had a few too many ding-dong battles with big fish—or big snags, for that matter—you will assuredly have pulled all the stretch out of your monofilament, but by the same token you will also have pulled the elasticity out of it, and some of the strength. It pays to replace a monofilament line after a few real heavy outings.) Now the new American woven or braided polyester fibre line overcomes all these difficulties.

Many anglers tie a 'collar' of much stronger line next to the hook, to take the shock of casting—beach casting especially.

It's not a bit of good pontificating about hooks, leads and swivels, except simply to say this: buy the best. It's the cheapest part of the tackle, anyway, and penny-foolish is a real bad policy here. Hooks come in all shapes and sizes and you need a fair variety of sizes. Keep the points sharp with a slip of emery. Keep them oily.

Swivels are supposed to keep the twist out of lines, not to put them in—some thin-wire, cheap swivels are worse than useless, they are merely the convenient spot where corrosion starts to do its fell work, unseen by you. Buy good, stout swivels and keep them lubricated.

Weights are a matter of necessity—hateful necessity. You need just enough to keep your bait where the fish will find it—none when drift-lining in calm water, or very little; little enough beneath your float; any weight from an ounce to a pound when fishing on the bottom. Weights are sold in all shapes and sizes, like hooks, but a good sort is that which has wire grapnels sprouting out of the lead—holds the bottom well. (You only need this when fishing stormy surf.) However, we go into the question of the appropriate weight in some detail when discussing various fish and methods.

A note on clothing. There are no fixed fashions among fishermen, thank goodness, but drab-coloured stuff makes sense if you are going to get within sight of your quarry —as you sometimes do in rock fishing, and often in estuary fishing. Highly cheerful colours sometimes break out on the pier and in the boat, and of course they do no harm and probably cheer up the party.

You need to keep warm, and dry. It can be absolutely perishing on the beach and in the boat—far colder than you thought when you left home, inland. A real good strong windcheater top jacket is quite essential, more than half the time. With appropriate sweaters beneath. On the beach, if not in the boat, you sometimes need waterproof trousers, and you certainly need waterproof footgear —Wellington boots, even waders. The old sou'wester doesn't come that shape by accident—centuries of usage and hard practical lore have gone into it. It remains unbeatable. However, if it isn't actually pouring down, a bobbly woollen cap is snug and comforting and makes you feel mildy nautical, if not piratical. I fancy one of those peaky caps that make you look like a Nazi soldier down on his luck—you know the sort, ski-ing caps they used to be called: porters at Waterloo wear them now. They give fine protection, especially with side flaps that can be turned down to protect the ears and neck. An old towel worn round the neck is the best thing for keeping rain out. Gannex, though stiff as plywood, keeps out rain and wind wonderfully well and stands up to any amount of hammering. Those popular fine-textured lightweight anoraks are no bloody good at all: you want something really hard-wearing, sea fishing is murder on everything.

Don't think this is an ancient worn-out grandpa quavering. You just don't know how cold and wet you can get until you've passed a wintry day at or on the sea, in the wrong clothing. Be prepared.

While on the subject of comfort—what you eat and drink is entirely your business, but be sure you don't go short. The appetite you work up during a day's sea fishing has virtually no relation to your normal workaday appetite. Hot drinks are especially welcome. I personally enjoy having a fire going, on the sort of outing that permits of it —and especially if I'm with a mate who can give a hand. But if you're not making it a cook-out, at any rate take a thermos full of soup and another full of your favourite tipple. Booze is most agreeable, of course, but a bit of a delusion. You only feel warmer for a little while. The booze sends the blood coursing through the outer vessels; there, shortly afterwards, it catches cold. But heaven forfend that I should separate a man from the comfort of his flask.

Chapter III

THE G.P. AND THE SPECIALIST

I fancy that most anglers are general practitioners rather than specialists. True, there is an increasing number of specialists—men who with single-minded dedication pursue bass, or tope, or sharks, or cod, or bream, or mullet, or skate, or conger, or the smaller delicious flat fish. This is all very well; once you have done a few years of fairly casual angling, catching whatever comes to hand, you may indeed think how nice it would be to turn your attention to one particular species. You are free to do so. But a book aimed at the needs of the beginner, I think, ought to give you some general indication of how to go about employing certain *methods*, rather than how to go about catching certain species. You can always specialise later.

So I am going to give you general instructions on how to employ your gear in certain situations. What you will catch, depends on what is there to be caught. If that sounds like the most obvious generalisation you ever read, so be it. The simple fact is that when you hurl your lure out into the sea, any of a number of different species may take hold of it. This is true even of freshwater fishing; it is truer still, and by far, of the salt, the teeming and multitudinous main.

I gave a lot of agonised thought to this question of how I should approach your instruction (and agonised thought is very bad for anyone). You see, you can break it down into species, sorts of fish. Fair enough: but who's to say that when you present a lure to catch a bass, it won't be taken by a codling, a whiting, or even a dab? It may

well be. You may be fishing for flounders, and catch eels.
There isn't a rigid and mutually exclusive social system
among fish, which says, We eat only this bait presented
in this way. No fear. In fact, one of the particular joys of
sea angling is that you never really know what you are
going to catch. When the rod tip knocks sharply down,
or the float plunges into the translucent depths, or skitters
away along the surface, when the line held so delicately
in your fingers jerks and quivers—why, then, it could be
almost *anything* at the other end. True, some methods make
it, let us say, *likelier* that you will hook, if anything, a given
species. But that is about as far as I'd like to go, having,
like most of us, caught more fish by accident than by fell
design.

Therefore I am going to sketch out the appropriate
methods to use when fishing in the set of situations which
sea angling really does break down into: pier or jetty,
shore, rock, and boat, with a considerable sidelong look
at estuary fishing, which is quite another thing again
and which subsumes certain of the methods common
to the freshwater fisher and the rock fisher. I shall also have
a bit to say about spinning from time to time in each
section, since it is a method which can be used in virtually
every situation.

As for the different species, they will appear when it
seems appropriate. I hope they appear often enough for
you, when you're actually out there, rod in hand, tingling
with anticipation and excitement.

Chapter IV

PIER AND JETTY FISHING

I think it makes sense to begin with this, though it is perhaps the least exciting method, simply because it is the easiest and most popular.

But it can be exciting enough, in all conscience.

In a special way this is the perfect form of fishing for the beginner; in another way it is the most *un*suitable. It is great for the beginner because it takes him out over deep water on his own two feet. When he arrives at the end of the pier, or thereabouts, he is already standing over deep or deepish water—therefore he has no casting problem. And it is the casting problem which (for no good reason) puts the beginner off. So, if you are bothered about having to learn to cast your lure out, stroll along the pier instead. It is the superlative ease of access to deep water which makes the pier in one sense perfect.

Where it is rather unsuitable for the novice is that it tends to fix you with the old impression that sea fishing was something not wildly exciting, almost urban, done in company and done with stout gear out of proportion to the small fish usually caught. A man who has never fished anywhere else except off the end of a pier does not really know how wildly exciting the lonelier, more arduous forms of the sport can be.

Well, never mind. Some of us don't want to take too much trouble, some of us actually like the company of our fellow men. To such easy-going souls—and note I don't say they are *not* the salt of the earth—to such gregarious chaps, the pier is the place.

Not the most productive place, as a general rule, in terms of fish caught. But there are exceptions even to that rule, as indeed there are exceptions to every rule—that's one of the things fishing teaches us more surely than any other. Deal Pier produces some very fine specimen cod every winter. Some West Country piers—and even Bournemouth—produce some very good bass from time to time. And all piers produce fish. But naturally, there being a certain amount of to-and-fro and hubbub and conviviality associated with a pier, not to mention boats coming and going, it follows that high summer and the pinnacle of the holiday season are not just the best times to fish.

But when a making tide—an incoming tide—coincides with early morning, or evening, then even the most popular pier can produce good sport. And in the off season you can sometimes have it almost to yourself. On some piers you may fish at night, on others you are not permitted to. If there is one thing you dare say about fishing without fear of instant flat contradiction, it is that night fishing is more likely to produce good catches (other things being equal) than day fishing.

Overhead casting is prohibited on many piers, for the sake of the casual passer-by who does not greatly fancy being impaled by a flying great hook adorned with segments of worm, or stunned by half a pound of lead. You can quite see the point of this prohibition. But wherever you go on piers, you see anglers doing their level best to get their bait as far away from the pier as they possibly can. A human aspiration, but *so* misguided. The beauty of pier fishing —some curmudgeonly parties will say its only attraction— is that it cuts out the need for casting altogether.

For consider: what is a pier? Look at it at low water. Take a cruise around it in a little boat. Climb down the lattice-work and rub your nose in the underwater construction. What do you see? Why, you see an abundance, an infinitude of fish food, all clinging to the piles! Why go further? The piles and girders are sure to be heavily festooned with weedy marine growths; and the weedy growths are heavily infested with marine life, a teeming population of small organisms on which small fish love to prey; and apart from the infested weed growths, the piles and girders and beams are sure to be encrusted with molluscs. Molluscs, my friend—luscious crackly stuff that costs you good money at the fishmonger's, when you can get it—lovely stuff like mussels. All this goodly grub attracts small fish—and small fish attract big fish. One of the cardinal rules of fishing for predatory fish is this—get among the small fish, if you can—for they are bait for the big fish.

Now you will see why there is no need to get your bait away from the pier. The fish are literally under your feet! Just lower away, vertically. There are exceptions to this, and we shall come to them in a minute, but by and large, just lower away.

Lower away *what?* Your float tackle, your paternoster, your flowing leger. Lovely terms, their origins lost in the mists of antiquity.

A paternoster rig is perhaps *the* basic terminal tackle for the static pier fisher. In essence, it simply means that your weight is tied right at the very end of your line, so that it goes down to the sea bed, touching it first. Now just a little way above that lump of lead you fix something called a *boom*, which stands out roughly at right angles to the vertical line, and on the end of which you tie your hook.

That is the basic principle of the paternoster. In practice there is plenty of room for variation. Sometimes the boom is a slip of rigid plastic, with a swivel immediately above and below the line end, and a trace and hook tied to the

12. Running leger rig.

11. **Twin-hook** paternoster tackle.

outboard end. But that is becoming rather uncommon. A simple method is to have a three-way swivel tied in the line, about a yard above the lead. The line to the reel is tied to the top eye of the swivel, the line to the weight is tied to the bottom eye, and the trace is tied to the middle eye which is at right angles to the other two. This is quite the simplest method. But you will find in any marine tackle shop a brass wire paternoster rig which takes the place of that single swivel and which has the virtue of making sure the hook length or trace stands well out from the reel line. This helps to prevent the trace getting wound round the reel line while you are making your cast.

There is nothing to stop you having two booms and two traces if you wish.

Fishing the paternoster is simplicity itself. You simply let the weight take the line off the reel, controlling its *run* with a finger or thumb, until you feel the weight hit the bottom. You then put the check on the reel, rest the rod against the railing, and wait until something bends the rod tip. It's very restful, of course. You will certainly get along well with a simple centre-pin reel, in fact it will suit you best. To while away the tedium, some anglers still use one of those jolly little bells, clipped to the rod tip, to wake them up when something happens. And why not, if it gives pleasure? A slightly more awake method is to take a bit of the reel line in your fingers and wait for a pluck at it. Your fingers are quite the most sensitive instruments you are likely to acquire.

The leger tackle is a variation of this static procedure. In this case your line is threaded through the weight —or through the brass ring which protrudes from the weight. The hook is duly tied on to the end of the line. Now the weight is 'stopped' about a yard or even two yards from the weight—some simply clip a half-moon lead over the line to act as a stop, some I've seen even using a

65

split shot, but that needs a deal of pinching on if it is to hold its place. In fact, it is far better to use a swivel as the stop. In this case you tie your hook to one end of a piece of monofilament about a yard long, and a swivel to the other end. You then pass your reel line through the weight, and tie it to the top eye of the swivel.

The leger has this advantage over the paternoster —when a fish takes hold, it can move away without much resistance. With a paternoster, the moment it takes your bait it must feel the anchoring power of that lump of lead. With the leger, it has at any rate a few feet of slack before the line, running through the eye of the weight, tautens up against the reel check. I personally have a notion that the leger is a more sensitive rig than the paternoster and a better method of hooking fish.

But if it has an advantage, so surely it has a drawback. The bait is lying absolutely on the sea bed. Now this is all very well, since you are by definition Bottom Fishing, with a vengeance. But on the actual bottom of the ocean there roams a creature called the crab. The crab in crab salad is a virtuous beast indeed, none more so, but the crab that roams the ocean floor nibbling at baits meant for fish is not as a rule—in fact, not *ever*—the luscious sort you see in salads. They are usually miserable little greenish things, in-edible and a thorough nuisance. You don't always suffer from their depredations, but when you do, it can turn an honest man into a monster of depravity in short order.

Happily there is a remedy for this sad state of affairs. If you find yourself suffering from the attentions of beastly little bait-robbing crabs, take that cork out of your pocket which you have craftily carried for this very purpose, and slip it on the trace a few inches above the hook. I should make that razor-blade cut half-way through the cork at home, at leisure, if I were you. Nasty when you do it on the pier and cut it right through, and not a spare in sight.

The cork will keep your lure just nicely up out of the reach of the crabs, and you have a quite effective rig working for you now.

I'm not absolutely mad keen on either of these tried and trusted methods myself, but more people use them than use any other methods, and they can't all be wrong. When you are fishing down from a high pier you pretty well have to stick to them: there's practically no way out. Legering and paternostering are vertical with a vengeance: they are highly economical of elbow room, and elbow room is often at a premium on a really popular pier. But if there is a lower stage of the pier to which you have the right of access, bringing you down much nearer to the surface of the water, then you can profitably indulge in float fishing and a variation of drift-lining, both of which are more sensitive and more productive, on the whole. And more fun.

True, you can use both these methods from the top level of a high pier. It's just that they don't work quite so easily, you have to work harder at it, you are not so closely in touch with your gear and therefore with your bait. But it can be done.

There are several valid variations of float fishing from a pier. At least three. You can combine float fishing with legering and with the paternoster, and you can float fish almost as if you were fishing in the canal at home.

To involve a float in your legering or paternostering will almost or quite certainly mean the use of a sliding float. Obviously, if the depth of water is greater than the length of your rod, and it surely will be, then you can't fix your float at the appropriate depth on the line and chuck it out. What you do is fix a *stop* on your reel line at the appropriate distance from the bottom or terminal tackle—a distance slightly greater than the depth of the water, and *that* you have to estimate, if you haven't surveyed the ground earlier, by dropping in a plummet—a weight tied to the end of the line. This stop is a bit of nylon, or valve rubber, about a quarter of an inch long, tied in to the line with a clove hitch. In the old days it used to be a bristle. Your line then passes through the middle of the sliding float, or through top and bottom rings which stand off at right angles from the body of the float. You heave the whole load over the side, the weight runs to the bottom, the float slides up the line till it reaches the stop. And stops. Easy.

Using a sliding float with a paternoster, make sure that the paternoster is free to run. Ensure this desirable state of affairs as follows. Tie your weight to one eye of a swivel, by a bit of monofilament about a yard long, at most. Pass the reel line through the other, or top, eye of the swivel and tie it immediately to one eye of another swivel. To the remaining eye of this second swivel, tie the hook trace —a good yard long, more if you fancy it streaming away in the current. Now, when a fish takes hold of your bait, he can run with the line—and your float will be the first to know.

I make a bit of a thing of this because with the standard brass-wire paternoster rig which I mentioned a little while ago, though certainly it ensures that your hook trace stands out well away from your reel line, it does mean that the fish gets no free run—he is up against the resistance of the weight as he moves with the bait.

Similarly with the float-leger method, make sure that on taking the bait the fish is free to move away before he comes up against a lot of resistance. The float must be the first to know—otherwise you might as well not bother with a float.

But of course there is another way of float fishing, a very free and ancient and exciting way. And that is simply to fish your float in what is called 'mid water', meaning

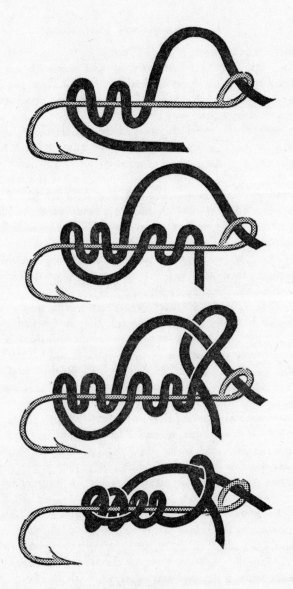

13. Knot for tying hook to trace.

anywhere between a foot off the bottom and a foot from the top. The reel line goes straight down through the float rings (exactly as in freshwater fishing) to the hook, and various weights as may be found necessary are nipped on the line a little way above the hook. You can of course incorporate a swivel between float and hook, and in fact it is a fairly good idea, if only because it helps to cut out some of the dreaded line twist when you have a fish fighting at the end of the line. And a swivel is a very convenient place on which to hang clip-on leads. All true: but don't forget, will you, that every swivel means two knots, and every knot means a weakening of the manufacturer's stated breaking strain of the line. Not that this often matters: 80 per cent of stated breaking strain is more than enough, in most cases. But tie a really careful double- or treble-half-blood every time.

This 'mid-water' float fishing is terrific, and I much prefer it to leger or paternoster, if only because you've got something to look at apart from the rod tip, it's lively and pretty and less static. But—you mustn't forget that the float will wander in the current, or tide, and while this may be exactly what you want it to do, it may not please your neighbours over-much if they happen to have their gear anchored firmly, and vertically, to the bottom, and you get caught up in it. This is another reason why free-ranging mid water float fishing, like drift-lining, is best done from the lower levels of the pier, if you can get there without getting either arrested or severely injured, or even drowned.

Near slack water, which means the odd half-hour at most when the tide is pretty well full and reluctant to turn and start all over again, in calm weather you can float fish happily right in close to the pier. Experiment with with various depths—start shallow, with the float only a yard or so above the hook, and, if you get no response, move the float up a little at a time until you are fishing on the sea bed. This is the only state of tide which allows you to fish the float almost as you would in a lake or canal. At other times the movement of the tide will sweep your float gear along, and either you will have to cast continually out away from the pier, fishing a short stretch as it returns, then casting out again, or, taking the opposite stance, you will be able to stream your float gear in the current, out and away from the pier.

This is just what you want to do when the mackerel shoals come inshore and create their usual wild excitement.

True, they are among the best of fish, both for eating and for the sport they provide—if you use appropriate tackle. Yet I cannot quite understand why the cry goes up 'the mackerel are in', while other summer fish seem not to provoke the same excitement. The garfish, that long-snouted, thin bodied, streamlined fighter which is usually or at least often around when the mackerel appear, is if possible an even finer fighter, dashing and leaping like a rainbow or sea trout. Many people seem to believe that the garfish is inedible, probably because of those funny bones, which do turn green when the fish is steamed or boiled; but in fact the flesh is very good eating, as despised foreigners know quite well. It is less oily than the mackerel's, but no less palatable.

Float fishing in this mode, swimming the bait at all sorts of depths from two feet to quite near the bottom, will serve to catch mackerel and garfish when they are swimming around off the pier. Drift-lining comes into its own in the same circumstances. For this you need nothing but a swivel about a yard from your hook, and a lead clipped on to the top eye of the swivel, or a half-moon lead folded over the line to nip that top eye tightly. You merely drop the bait and weight into the water, at your feet almost, and let the current take it away. It will sink, of course, but not too far.

You keep in constant touch with it by stopping the reel every few moments—when you clamp down on the reel, the weight and bait naturally rise in the water, an undulant swaying movement which adds greatly to its attractiveness, making it all so natural and lazy. I may say that this trick of trapping the reel every so often pays well when you are drifting the float, too—every time you stop the line being taken off the reel, up comes the bait to search a new layer of water. Then you release it and off it goes again, steadily but slowly sinking until you brake again.

Either with the float, or merely with the drifting weight and bait, you are in constant touch and will feel a knock, even if you see nothing. Perhaps this drift-lining is *the* most effective method of bait fishing in a current flow —there is virtually nothing to alarm the fish or rouse its natural suspicions, everything is simple, and streamlined and cunning, you feel the touch and *whoosh*, you clamp everything solid and swing the rod top back firmly and swiftly. And you feel the fish kicking on the end of it all. It's a strange and exhilarating feeling.

Mullet approach some piers in high summer, and it is almost irresistible, at any rate to some natures, to try for them. But the mullet is a desperately crafty fish, not exactly shy, I'd say, but supernaturally cautious and fastidious, and to catch them regularly is really among the most difficult exercises in the sport. Stealth and fine tackle are prime necessities for mullet—and since mullet grow big and burly, fine tackle can mean frustration, fish hooked and lost. (A mullet's mouth is very soft, and if you rough them up the hook hold gives way all too readily.) But stout tackle means that you never get a chance, anyway. So there you are. It's not much use trying to catch mullet when the pier is crowded; quietude is called-for. You may have a chance early and late—especially late, on those piers which allow night fishing. Likelier, though, I fancy, from a small harbour jetty than from a populous seaside-resort pier. You can fish for them with ordinary roach tackle, but a good compromise is that sort of middleweight coarse fishing rod known as the Avon style. In fact this is a perfect rod for the sport. With a centre-pin reel loaded with something like five-pound breaking-strain line, you can send your float subtly down the current, with a fragment of almost anything on the hook, fishing it merely two feet below the surface, and trying ever-greater depths until you get among them. A scrap of tiny ragworm is as good as anything, but mullet have been caught on all sorts of bait—even macaroni! They certainly eat bread—and cheese. But sticking to marine worms and bits of fish makes sense.

Some anglers in the West Country even fish for herring from harbour walls and jetties, at the appropriate season —preferably fishing by night, with a bit of ragworm on light float tackle suitable for roach, fishing fairly deep.

A word about floats. The floats one sees used in the sea are a striking and multifarious lot, but generally speaking they are bright and they are big. Too big, I often think. True, you need to see your float, but never think that the sea fish is an idiot. If the fish feels the resistance of the float as it is drawn down through the water, that fish has (generally speaking and with a few exceptions) enough sense to realise that there is something fishy going on and to release the lure smartly. The big bung habit dies hard, but really a fat 'pike float', which is what you so often see in use, really isn't the most intelligent approach to sea fish. (It isn't the most intelligent approach to pike either, come to that.) Try to select a float which is above all *slim*, a float which offers the least possible resistance to being drawn down through the water. Often it will have to be a big and buoyant float, capable of carrying a load of lead and of being seen in the roily sea:

but it should be slender for its length. The old goosequill threaded through a length of cork or balsa wood, the whole thereafter nicely painted and varnished, is as good as anything. But of course there are lots of plastic floats available, if you don't enjoy making your own—a delightful pastime for the murky winter evenings, I may say; sometimes better by far than watching the box.

Not everyone knows it, but there is a cunning device known as the self-hooking float, which is bound to appeal to some mentalities. This is a good slender float with a wide circular disc of stiff plastic sheet, two to three inches in diameter, slipped down over the top quill or pinnacle of the float, and glued in position. The theory is that an eager-biting fish—such as the mackerel, pre-eminently—diving on the bait, pulls the flat of the float down on to or into the water, with a bang. The resistance so suddenly set up—and it really is a considerable resistance, as you can imagine—stops the hook short in its travel downwards. But since the fish is by then committed to its dive, the point enters and the fish is hooked without any assistance from the angler, who is assumed not to have noticed anyway. Striking a quick bite at a distance really is a bit of a problem; co-ordination of eye and hand, the dear old reflexes, can't always be relied upon to be adequate to the demands of the moment.

Then there is the natural elasticity of the line, and the big 'bag' of line in the water, and wind resistance . . . you can go on elaborating the factors which make for missed bites. The self-hooking float helps to eliminate some of them. Still, it feels like cheating—to some of us fastidious nuts.

Bass and pollack, two of our greatest medium-weight sporting fish, may be caught from suitable piers in summer, in fact any time between April and early October, depending on where you are and what the weather is like—and *has* been like, months previously. With the coming of winter, the pier is used mainly by cod and whiting fishermen, in a general sense, but there is always the odd flat fish to be hoped for. Fishing on the bottom, certainly, is the thing for the winter months—not much use fishing mid-water then, for there won't be many fish swimming at that level, nor anywhere near the surface.

Spinning can be indulged in, provided you have access to one of the lower platforms. Like drift-lining and mid-water float fishing, it can really *only* be practised from a platform near the water level: from the top storey you should only expect to fish vertically, on the bottom. I will be going into spinning techniques fairly thoroughly later on, when we come to rock fishing and estuary fishing, so I'll say no more about it here.

The pier fisherman's baits are about as varied as his quarry, and it really does pay to notice what is popular in a given district—or even to ask. One thing is pretty sure—where there is a pier, a bait salesman won't be very far away. As a rule. Of course it is cheaper to dig your own ragworms and lugworms, but the time factor, not to mention the energy factor, militates against this healthful pursuit for many of us. I should guess that an absolute majority of pier fishermen use lugworm as a bait. It's all right, of course—often it's the best there is. But don't forget that fish are the greatest fish-eaters in creation. Strips of mackerel or herring are always useful, the fleshy parts of crustaceans, prawns and shrimps, sandeels, small fish entire, pieces of squid, razor fish, mussels—there is practically no end to the list of fishy baits. Don't forget that a useful bait for bass is a piece of kipper. Yes, honestly. It's strange that some fish, not especially nice to know, are very finicky about fresh bait—conger, for example —while some fish which are simply pure and fresh and shining (and exquisite to eat) will gobble up pretty stale

14. Ragworm on long-shanked hook.

and stinky old stuff. Pilchards attract bass, by the way.

Soft crab is a great bait, but obtaining it is not so easy.
It is when a crab has just thrown his old hard shell, having
outgrown it, that he is tender and especially attractive
to other creatures. But to find soft or 'peeler' crabs is an
art in itself. However, ask around. A really obliging (or
even rapacious) local dealer may get you some, but you
may have to buy a lot of beer.

Some people fish for flounders with maggots. In estuaries,
at any rate. But I've never seen it happen on a pier.

Earthworms die rather quickly in sea water.

Mackerel prefer mackerel. They really do. Actually I
do most of my mackerel fishing elsewhere, but if I were on a
pier and the mackerel were 'in' I'd back little bright
strips cut from the side of one of their own brethren to
equal or beat any other bait. Problem: what do you catch

76

the first mackerel on, before you can start using mackerel as bait for mackerel? Answer, a sprat. They love sprats. It is in pursuit of vast shoals of sprats, or sandeels, or pilchards, that they come close inshore in summer.

When the mullet are right on the surface it isn't a lot of use to offer them conventional fishy or 'natural' baits. I think I mentioned macaroni. Bread is also reasonably effective. ('If they won't eat bread, give them cake', said Marie Antoinette. Or almost. I have approached this state by mixing custard powder in my bread paste, just as I do ashore. I don't know that it made it work any better. A bit of floating bread crust I once saw do considerable execution when fished from a jetty in the West Country. But since I was standing alongside the floating crust expert, and catching them lower down in the water on bits of ragworm, I'm not sure what that proved.) But I *do* fancy that a touch of pilchard oil mixed with the bread paste really pays off. So far as anything can be said to pay off in this branch of fishing. Mullet are real worthwhile targets: they can tax the patience of a saint, yet on occasion they can give great rewards. I'm not too happy about including them in this pier fishing chapter, but hedge a bit because I *did* say pier or jetty, and while the seaside resort pier may not be much of a mullet ground, the jetty, especially within a harbour, very often is.

Generally speaking, it's the old flatfish, cod and whiting in winter, and bass, pollack and mackerel in summer. A pier's not a bad place to begin, perhaps, if you love the human race.

Chapter V

BOAT FISHING

Nothing will keep me out of a boat, given half a chance to get in; but nothing will make me recommend boat fishing to anyone else, either in private or in public. The responsibility is just too awful. I can't face it.

If you mean to go out on the sea in a boat, on your own head be it. The sea is a really dangerous place. You only have to look at the papers or switch on the radio to learn all about that. It is simply marvellous to be at sea, in conditions which you are capable of enjoying: but it would be irresponsible to urge any beginner to put to sea without proper professional or at any rate experienced guidance.

Go to sea by all means. We're not the island race for nothing. Sea fishing from a boat, even quite close inshore, is superbly enjoyable (when you're not sick or terrified, that is). It opens up horizons which are denied to the land-lubber. But lub away, be a lubber and proud of it, unless you know someone, or can hire someone, who is really a master of the trade and thoroughly capable. The sea changes as the weather changes—and sometimes before the weather changes. It is OK one minute and you're in trouble the next. I am no great shakes as a boat-handler myself, though I can cope after a fashion and have owned several sailing boats, and crewed in many more. But I couldn't begin to write a manual which would teach you how to stay safe while at sea, and therefore I am simply going to say this—don't go to sea in a boat unless you know what you're doing or alternatively have someone with you who does. Who *really* does.

Having said that, as in duty bound, let me say that fishing from a boat is dreamy, man, dreamy. Not only does it open up those new horizons I spoke about, in the fishing sense, but there you are, secluded in a world of your own, absolutely on your tod, free from the workaday world and the frets of 'longshore life. It's heavenly.

Needless to say you only go out in a boat when the weather is set fair. It then gives you the opportunity of getting out over various 'marks', as they are called, where fish tend to congregate. Nothing could be farther from the truth than the naïve notion that fish are distributed more or less equally or at random throughout the illimitable ocean. Far from it. Fish congregate, just as people congregate ashore. There are vast tracts of empty ocean and often you feel you've covered most of them. But when you get over the right mark, you know. You start catching 'em.

How, then, do you find these right marks, where fish are congregated? That's just it. The first thing to do is to ask questions of the local talent; the second thing to do is watch them. Every district has its favourite marks. You can't keep a good mark dark. I can't tell you where they are in your chosen locality, though I know where they are in mine.

Good marks or grounds vary greatly. What attracts fish in the first place? Well, for one thing, other fish do —but this is not at all a matter of marks. Mackerel, for example, follow shoals of sprats and sand eels. So do herrings. Larger fish also chase shoals of small fish. These are drifting or travelling 'marks', not really static marks at all. Wheeling screaming gulls will often tell you where the slaughter is taking place. You hurry there. But local knowledge will often reveal the expected path of the shoals. In these cases you simply prospect around until you find the feeding fish, following the signs. Often you actually see the disturbance on the surface of the water —when it is reasonably calm, of course. But the birds will spot it first.

But marks proper, ground marks: marks geographical, marks immemorial, marks immutable . . . These may be areas of sand, areas of rock, or areas of wreck. All three come as welcome interruptions to the tedious uniformity of the sea bed's vast expanse of mud, pebbles, and rubbish; and fish of various sorts love them.

Rocks first: why should a rocky area attract fish to congregate? Plainly, because where there are rocks there is food adhering to those rocks, and shelter within the fissures and crevices of those rocks. Rocks come in at least two different categories: ground rocks, and so-called pinnacle rocks, which are rocks that rise quite steeply from the sea bed almost to the surface. Normally you will find these precipitous rock formations only when you are fishing well out from the coast in deep water. They are all known by repute, but you will probably be taken there, for money, by an experienced professional skipper, who may well use an echo sounder to locate the rock tips.

Some of the very greatest fishing available to us is to be had out around these sea-bed mountains. The trawler has to steer clear, which means that fish inhabit these ridges and gullies almost unpursued—except by their own kind. It is in this environment—though not only or exclusively in this environment—that you may take great conger, skate, rock cod, ling, coalfish; very fine pollack, tope and dogfish, mackerel and whiting, bream and—shark . . . In a way it is the cream of fishing. Alas, I simply cannot just bluntly recommend it to the beginner, though if your stomach is strong and your purse reasonably well filled, you will get more thrills and learn more in one day out with a professional skipper than all the books in the British Museum could teach you in a lifetime.

15. Lugworm on hook.

Go, then: hire a skipper, or rather share his boat; take your gear or hire his; live and learn. If not prone to sea-sickness you will have the time of your life. But since it is deep-sea fishing, I really can't go into it seriously in a book for beginners. For beginners have no place out there, except in the care of skippers who can look after them and teach them far more than any book.

But closer in, within sight of the shore—yes, with proper care, you can have some splendid fishing. I'm sorry, honestly, to keep on grizzling about this safety factor, it's so un-English and prissy: but when you've been in the trade of so-called communications as long as I have, you get quite nervous about advocating anything interesting which can kill or maim your readers, and boat fishing certainly can do that, and will, if you don't behave rationally. So learn about boat management and about the ways of the sea before you venture forth, or go as passenger to someone who really knows. Sorry. Not another word.

Inshore boat fishing undoubtedly provides better sport, taking this month with that month and bad times with good, than pier fishing. I wouldn't say that it provides better sport, year in year out, than beach casting and rock fishing, but there is always this nice tingly feeling that you never know what will take your bait next. This is far more the case in boat fishing than in fishing from the shore, I think. One minute you are hooking bream, the next minute a pollack takes your bait; luscious flatfish may be varied by wretched little pout; a great sharky tope may snap your mackerel off the hook as you reel in. You may catch bass, conger, rays or even sea trout. And so on. Infinite variety, infinite expectation: it keeps you on the *qui vive* and incidentally, if that interests you, it opens your eyes pretty wide to the abundance and variety and the sheer total inexplicability of the all-mighty Providence that is keeping you supplied with the fruits of creation. But never mind about the metaphysics: they're a physic not everyone can swallow.

The inshore boat fishing we are rambling on about just now is the sort you might do in a dinghy, that is to say a hairy little boat without any living accommodation, without decking, just an open boat such as you get shipwrecked in, if your luck holds. No cabin, as a general thing, no shelter and no cooking facilities and no loo. It may be propelled by oars, which is laborious to a degree you simply wouldn't believe, until you try it, or by an outboard engine, which is all right, or by an inboard engine, which is lovely, so long as somebody else maintains it—properly.

It may or may not have the assistance of a bit of a mast and a scrap of sail, but the less you the angler have to do with sail, the better. The joys of sailing are a heaven in themselves, and I've always found it very difficult to choose between sailing and fishing. I don't know that they mix too well, though. Still, my old friend Jake, the black-a-vised and piratical free lance who operates from Sunset Creek, he does all his fishing in a lugger with two masts and three sails, namely main, mizzen and lug, mate; he despises the infernal combustion engine with a religious fervour of contempt, and he as I say does all his fishing, which is plenty, under sail. Having been his crew on several fraught occasions—including night fishing for conger—I wish to recommend quite firmly that you do not rely entirely on the wind to get you home.

So you're out in a beamy, well-found dinghy or long boat or whatever it may be called in the locality (local names vary, including local names for fish, which often seem like a different language and in fact are just that). You are now about to discover the real joys of fishing for the furious fighting fish which, weight for weight, out-fight anything that swims in fresh water, outfight even the barbel, the trout and the carp.

To enjoy this sport, please use tackle that is appropriate. What are we after today? Let's say it's bass. The bass, we know, are 'in', and with luck they will do what is known as 'shoaling' about twice a day. The birds will lead your skipper to the spot where the fish are tearing in and out among swarms of brit (small fry). He manoeuvres the boat up-tide of the shoal and you drift your bait down to where the fury is going on. Ideally you should be spinning, casting a long narrow fluttering spoon ahead of you, tied to a trace of about 6 lb. breaking strain, connected via one swivel to your reel line. The effectiveness of the spinner seems to be governed to some extent by the current average size of the natural small fish which the bass are hunting. It always pays to carry a variety of sizes, but start off big.

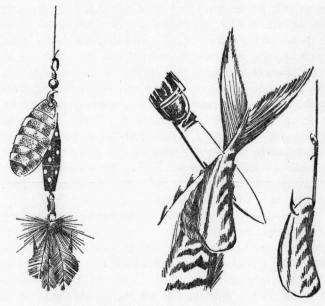

16. (*Left*) Bar-spoon with feathers.
17. (*Right*) Cutting a 'lask' of mackerel for hook bait.

This surely is the best fun, I think, but if you don't fancy spinning you may drift your hook, baited with a silvery strip or 'lask' cut from near a fresh mackerel's belly, with one small weight on the swivel. You can drift the float down if you like, but it isn't actually necessary, though some of us greatly enjoy watching a float. Occasionally when the surface activity fades away you may still keep in contact with the bass by going deeper, but more often you have to move on. The excitement won't last a terrible long time anyway, which is the reason why it pays to go out with a skipper who knows what he's doing.

You have to make fairly long casts at this game—bass won't stand being sailed over.

Bream, which are strictly local in distribution, give great sport and make good eating. Black bream abound in the English Channel, and can be found elsewhere than at the celebrated centres of Bognor Regis and Littlehampton. You won't be spinning for bream, but fishing a bait well off the bottom. How far off the bottom, it is up to you to discover. One way of finding out is to rig up a paternoster, bait your hook with worm or mackerel strip, and lower away gently until you feel your lead touch the bottom. Don't let everything go slack—hold it taut there for a minute or three. Then quietly raise it, reeling in briskly a few turns at a time, and then resting it for a couple of minutes. By this method you can search the whole depth from right on the sea bed to near the surface. When you start getting bites, note the depth and keep to it. Bream fight like furies. A six to eight pound breaking strain line, and a suitably flexible rod, will make it a sporting contest.

A great many anglers use float tackle when fishing for black bream, and it's OK so long as you don't mind the constant reeling-in. And of course the drift-line technique works well in the sense that it enables your bait to cover a big area; but judging just how *deep* your bait is fishing, and varying this by adjusting the weight of lead, makes extra activity. Some like this; some like to relax. For big relaxers, paternosters or float paternoster techniques appeal.

Flat fish appeal greatly since they are so universally enjoyed at table. (Which is not quite true of some of the round fish. Bass, for example, are to my mind really delicious, with a delicate creamy flesh not dissimilar to salmon trout but perhaps a little more digestible—yet some people don't fancy them.) Sole, the queens of the lot, tend to live over soft sea beds—sand, mud, who can say? I'm not at all sure that anyone really and truly can put his hand on his heart and say 'I am going out especially to catch sole with rod and line—I know where to find them and what it takes'. Sole catching is, I'm rather inclined to think, a happy accident which occurs to you when you are simply fishing, fishing in hope, with a bait right on the bottom. You will probably catch sole as often from the shore as from a boat. They are certainly bottom feeders, and take worms, molluscs, shrimps. But the sole has an exceptionally small mouth, and to hook one you need to be using an exceptionally small hook. You want a chub or even roach size hook—No. 10 isn't ridiculous. So perhaps you *can* go fishing specially for soles —equipped with these tiny hooks and appropriately tiny bits of bait. But if you do, of course, you stand a fair chance of not hooking fish with larger mouths which take the bait you meant for the sole . . . It's a cruel dilemma, isn't it?

The plaice is a great friend and favourite of the inshore small boat angler, ever welcome, dead easy when you've found him. Plaice run about one to two pounds in weight on the average, but exceed this greatly on occasion—the record is nearer 8 lb. They can actually be caught almost all the year round and their distribution is very wide, but by and large they are reckoned as at their best in autumn and summer: in winter some of them, if not all, seem to go to deep water to spawn. Trawling did wholesale damage to many plaice grounds but there are still plenty left close inshore. They are much better fighting fish than you might imagine—on light tackle, a plaice will give you plenty to think about.

Plaice love shellfish and worms, and are bottom feeders. Working this out will give you a notion of where they may be sought. Answer—on sandy patches where worms are regularly coming and going in and out, and over shellfish beds which often break up such sandy tracts. The bait to use is what is available, of course, but lugworms, ragworms, razorfish, soft crabs, seem a better bet than strips of fish.

But if strips it must be (because you can't get anything else) don't despair. Plaice are not altogether immune to the crime of cannibalism. Quite a few have been hooked on spoons.

But as a general thing, prospecting and exploring a known good sea bed with a *moving* bait will probably get you best results. I must say I don't see the point of fishing with a stout rod and 20 lb. line, when the quarry is plaice. A carp rod, though much too long in a crowded boat, in fact quite vicious and anti-social, is just about right in power and scope. A short spinning rod of the kind known laughingly as 'a trout rod' is just the job—and those very short crank-handled rods, that take the closed-face fixed-spool reel so well, are ideal, if your arm muscles are up to the job of pumping a fish up from the bottom with the minimum of leverage to help you. But the usual run of seven or eight foot glass rod will serve you well, or your pike rod at a pinch.

I have taken part in some very static anchored plaice hunts, and they were moderately productive and moderately sickening. (It's always more sickening when you're anchored.) I think you *should* anchor, when prospecting a plaice ground, but that doesn't mean you need be content to chuck your bait overboard and rest on your oars. Plaice nose around quite a lot, and the consensus of informed opinion seems to be that a bait has more chance of attracting a plaice if it is on the move—not dramatically: a plaice isn't one of your piratical predators which spends its time dashing around after prey; but gently on the move. This seems to be especially the case in respect of vertical movement—if you can get your bait rising and falling in the water, the plaice seems to want to investigate it.

One way of doing this is to feed your tackle over the stern and stream it away gently in the water, sinking all the time of course and being carried downstream from the boat by the tide. Eventually you stop paying line off the reel, eventually the old equation works itself out and the weight bumps the bottom. You feel this quite distinctly. (If you don't, you haven't got enough weight on to get it down in the stream. Put more on.) When the bait is on the bottom, reel in gently but firmly, very slowly but evenly, at the same time raising the rod tip. (This is where the long rod comes in, of course.) Keep on reeling in and periodically raise and lower the rod.

Chances are that you will feel the quivering pluck of the plaice bite. Take no notice. Just go on reeling gently in. Either you'll suddenly feel the solid weight of the fish 'on', self-hooked, or you won't. But you probably will.

Whiting are not perhaps very 'sporting' fish, but all's grist, and if they were fished for with reasonably light tackle there would be fewer complaints on the score of their faint-heartedness. In autumn a big run-in of much larger whiting accompanies the run-in of cod, their close relatives, and since the cod angler often catches whiting of a pound or two on a thirty-pound line meant for cod, well, naturally he feels a bit let-down. But whiting taken on plaice tackle are all right. They are rather greedy fish, fond of fish above all else, and they are bottom feeders best angled for with a paternoster, I think. A flowing leger is effective in itself, but it depends how clean the bottom is. If it is roughish, a paternoster ending in a pear-shaped lead may be less susceptible to being 'hung up'. (But everything you put overside gets hung up one time or another.)

Of course there is nothing to prevent you from using two or even three booms and hooks on a paternoster. This distributes your bait vertically in the water and doubles or trebles your chance of hooking something. Naturally, if you do get two or three fish 'on' at once, and it is by no means rare when fishing for gregarious fish like whiting and mackerel, then of course you do need a stoutish line and a stoutish rod. Or let me put it another way round. If you fancy the use of really light tackle, good man, but use only one hook. If you don't, or if you possess only rather stout tackle, why, then, make a virtue of necessity and use two or three links and hooks. Then you stand a good chance of really feeling you have a fight on your hands.

(I expect you will have worked it out for yourself that one objection to using heavy tackle, strong lines, is that the stout line itself has vastly more resistance *to the water* than a thin line. The tide really feels it and really pulls it. Hence, you are forced to use much heavier weights on a stout line than on a thin ['fine'] line. It all adds up.)

The pollack is a great favourite with boat fishers, and no wonder. It is a real hearty thumper, the pollack, and runs up to jolly good weights. Fish of 20 lb. have been known, but you will more likely hit one between a pound or two and four or five, at which weight, on suitable gear, he will open your eyes for you. I suppose the South-west has most pollack, but really they seem to turn up pretty well everywhere. I wouldn't like to say what sort of sea bed they really favour, for although supposed to be rock lovers, and very frequently taken near rocks, they do turn up elsewhere, in the open sea over sand and grit, even over shingle. You can catch them from spring to early winter, for sure.

The pollack is also rather delightfully easy-going about the depth at which he works. Thus, although believed to be a bottom feeder—and it *does* feed a great deal on the bottom—yet it is often taken by spinning in mid-water, by drift-lining and even by swimming a float down-tide. I think the one thing we can say with some confidence about the pollack is that it likes to be up and doing, on the go, a-chasing something nice.

Thus, although you may well interest the odd fish on our static rig, leger or paternoster, you are many times more likely to interest one if your bait is moving. In fact the pollack is a fish that can be angled for excitingly with spinning gear, including the device known as 'feathers', so often used for mackerel, with the glittering 'jig' lure that you work up and down in the water, and with the curiosity known as a plug. I am very fond of fishing the plug. This is a light lure shaped somewhat like a fish, and not a true spinner since it never revolves. Instead of spinning vanes, it has a lip-vane at the front which when dragged through the water causes it to dive, flutter, and wobble in a rather life-like way. Plugs come solid and jointed, and the ones to go for are the jointed ones, which have a mighty seductive sinuous shimmy and wobble. A Hawaiian grass-skirt dancer has nothing on it for seductiveness. At least, pollack seem to think so. But a spoon will do nicely.

Otherwise you can go drift-lining, or float fishing, varying the depth from time to time. Fish strips work, worms at a pinch, but *the* pollack lure pre-eminently is the live sand eel. If you can get it. Fishermen in the West, certainly, supply them, in exchange for filthy lucre. Those rubber strips known as artificial sand eels are used, but I can't say I've as much faith in them as in a long bright fluttering strip cut from the belly and side of a mackerel.

The great stand-by for all boat fishing is the mackerel. As bait, I mean.

As quarry, too, the mackerel is in a class of its own. When they are in they are in, when they are on the feed they are simply suicidal. They go raving mad. They fight like little tigers, they make wonderful grub. From late spring or early summer right through to autumn, you can find them almost anywhere. The mackerel never lets you down. And perhaps the very finest way of fishing for it is from a little boat.

When, in the early summer, mackerel really settle

18. Roller rod-tip for heavy boat work.

down to feed on the vast travelling shoals of herring fry, pilchard fry, sprats and sand eels, you can catch them absurdly easily on almost anything bright and fishy. The only way to make this holocaust reasonably sporting is to use light tackle—though, of course, as I said before, if you don't own light tackle, you can more or less make up for it by using two or three hooks, or even more, and catching several fish at a go. But it just isn't the same, not really.

If you are fishing one hook only, then a light rod really is necessary if you are to get the indescribable feel of the thing. I think I have said that I fished for mackerel with a two-pound breaking-strain line. Since the mackerel rarely exceeds two pounds in weight, that seems all right. But of course I wouldn't recommend going so light—four or five pounds is OK, six or seven quite permissible if you are going to use several hooks—including that strange device the 'string of feathers', a sort of crude 'fly' sold specially for mackerel, though quite effective on pollack as well.

Genuine fly fishing with a fly rod and fly line and big gaudy sea trout flies is quite possible, I've done it more than once, but of course only a synthetic fly line can stand up to the ravages of salt water, the nice old silk line dies the death *instanter*. And the fly is only effective on the surface. Better your chances with the spinning rod and a small flashy spinner—this is the greatest fun. The whirling blade type of spinner known as the bar spoon is probably best of all, but Devon minnows work wonders. But there is just nothing a mackerel likes better than a silvery strip of . . . mackerel! Drifting a hook baited with a strip of mackerel, spinning a small lively bright lure, trailing a sand eel or even a worm . . . What will *not* attract this predacious little hunk of heart? Precious little I know of. This is what makes mackerel fishing at once so wildly exciting and so fraught with dubiety—satiety sets in unless you deliberately restrict yourself to trout-strength tackle, and take them one at a time, sportingly. Unless you're a fish-hog, of course. Mackerel take at various depths, but generally they are pretty well in the top layer of the water. (But occasionally there are some very *big* ones right on the bottom!)

One aspect of small-boat fishing that never fails to amuse me, though perhaps I am too easily amused, is when the chaps afloat come almost ashore and cast landwards into the breakers, after bass. This is OK, of course, but when you see chaps standing on the tide line heartily casting *out* while chaps in boats are heartily casting *in*, you do wonder which of them is making the best of it. But there it is: in a boat properly handled, either at anchor, or with a good man *at the oars* to keep the boat just so, and make sure it doesn't get dashed ashore on a big wave, you can certainly get among the fish that feed in the turmoil created by surf—not only bass, but codling, too.

Chapter VI

ROCK FISHING

Fishing *from* rocks, that is, not *for* rocks. Not even for rocklings, which are funny looking little fish sporting beards, and sometimes virtually indistinguishable from television directors and sub-editors. There is the three-bearded rockling, the four-bearded rockling, and the five-bearded rockling: all small, drab and relentless in taking baits meant for better fish. (The 'beards', of course, are actually barbels. Anyone who has seen the freshwater fish called barbel knows what a barbel looks like. Gudgeon have them, too.)

Of course a great deal of first-rate fishing goes on from boats which venture into deep water and hang about near rocks rising from the sea bed. Yes, but this chapter is about fishing from rocks around the shore, fishing on your own two feet. Which had better be encased in something suitable, for clambering about on rocks is both wet and slippery. It's easy to keep out the wet and not too difficult to cope with the slipperiness, but the two necessities tend to clash.

Rubber boots are dry, but dangerous. Hobnails and studs are sensible, but you don't normally come across them in rubber boots. Every man to his own conclusion. I once fished with a chap who wore football boots. Eventually he broke his leg. Perhaps the best solution is to wear pukka game fisher's waders, the real M'Coy kind which are actually stocking waders, pulled on over your thick socks, and then topped off by brogues worn over *them*. Yes, nice, but expensive.

I spent one happy season wearing ex-Govt Surplus dispatch riders' knee boots, and old motor cycle riding breeches. Very effective: it takes a long time for the water to penetrate well-dubbined leather, with a good gusset-type tongue in the boots. On the whole, despite my present rheumaticky state, I still think it's better to concentrate on keeping your foothold and to hell with getting wet. One ardent rock fisher whom I knew wore nothing on his nether limbs but shorts and rope-soled sandals. His legs were a mass of bruises and abrasions, very ugly, but he seemed happy and rarely fell in, not what you'd call fell in.

Every time I start writing a new section of this book I find myself irresistibly drawn to saying 'This is the greatest fun'—because they all *are* great fun, I've enjoyed the lot. But really, I do think rock fishing is terrific sport, closely allied to game fishing ashore, with all that intimate feeling you get when you are so near to your quarry, plus the special delights of the ozone and spray and general sea-sense.

What you want, ideally, is a sort of ledge or rim of rocks that stand up proud of the high-water mark, and even prouder of low water; that is to say rocks that have a fair depth of water right up to them, rocks that go down almost or quite vertically into the water.

This is the ideal for productive fishing, but of course some of us have to manage, some of the time, according to where we happen to find ourselves, with jumbled rocks that are not arranged so neatly and conveniently—rocks that give on to a good fishing depth only at high water, rocks with gullies and channels between them, complex and broken wracky rocks. Well, they're all rocks, and given a decent depth of water when the tide is in, you'll do. But best of all the lovely sort of rock structure I described at the start. And there are plenty of rocks like that round the British Isles, though, perhaps naturally, they are commoner in the West than elsewhere.

Note particularly: if you have to climb down a cliff to get at your rocks, as well you may, make sure that you can climb back. Nuff said?

Mackerel, bass and pollack are the fish most fished for from rock stations such as these. (But sometimes you catch what you're not fishing for.) The best methods at your disposal, whatever species you may be hoping for, are spinning and float fishing. True, you may dangle a pater-noster in the water if you choose, thousands do, I dare say, and why not? But it does seem a bit of a waste of pleasure, and pleasure being rationed somewhat stringently, it seems a pity to waste any of it.

Yet there can be occasions when a paternoster with a trace that is free to run is obligatory. It all depends on the sea bed near the rocks. By and large, the fish that come as close inshore as this are hunting for food that grows and/or lurks in and around the crevices and surfaces of the rocks themselves, and the weeds that flourish thereabouts. Yes, but occasionally they are not actually interested in the rocks, but in the sea bed just off the rock wall—when that sea bed is covered by weed, or is composed of a rough stony bottom freely interspersed with weed growth.

Such territory harbours a great deal of food which fish enjoy, including of course crabs. If the bottom is very rough and bad, or if the weed growth is heavy—kelp beds can be truly dense—then you are almost forced to use a pater-noster with the terminal lead hanging down quite a way below the hook, a good foot or two and maybe even more. (Trial and error again, Jack.) Then your weight will go plummetting down to the bottom, but your bait will either rest lightly on top of the weed, or just nicely within it, or will toddle about in the swirl of water among the stones but not getting stuck in the crevices of the bottom. Crafty old anglers use a 'rotten bottom'—by which delightful term they mean that the line which connects the weight and the swivel is, well, not actually *rotten*, but so much weaker than the rest of the line that if the weight gets hung up, and you have to heave-O!, then it breaks first and you only lose your lead.

However, efficient as the paternoster may be, it is also less interesting than the float and the spinner. For float fishing in this situation, simply nothing is better than the carp rod aforementioned. It is just the right strength and weight to cast your bit of lead—an ounce at most, as a rule, even as little as half an ounce; and if the current is strong and you have to go to one-and-a-half ounces, it will still cope. It is light, and it reaches out nicely. And it will certainly handle the bass and pollack you get, and more than handle the mackerel. As I told you, I used nothing but a ten-foot sea trout fly rod for years, and though it flexed alarmingly at times, it was so thrillingly sensitive and responsive, a delight to handle. Stick to the slender float I recommended and you'll miss fewer bites. Adjust the float, up and down, until you hit on the depth at which fish seem to be taking.

Of course your beach casting rod, if you have one, will cope with the situation. What you need most is a certain degree of length—you are reaching out a bit over the water. At a pinch your pike rod will serve you, of course, or a seven-foot boat rod if it comes to that. Of course it will: you can improvise amazingly. But I'm trying to put you in touch with the maximal pleasure. For that is what fishing is all about: pleasure: otherwise we'd all be queue-ing at the fishmonger's.

Of course, the depth at which you fish your float bait, and even the manner in which you fish it, will depend somewhat on the style of rock formation you are fishing. It's all very nice to have a neat shelf poised over deepish water, everything laid on almost as nice and tidy as if you were back home fishing the canal. But sometimes all you have is a ragged formation of scattered rocks, reaching out to sea in a highly untidy fashion and nowhere giving you command of the depths. In this case you may have to manage by fishing little gullies where the water races and creams between individual rocks. You will have to fish very shallow, since the depth of water may be no more than a yard or two.

Initially you might think there couldn't be any point in fishing these little cuts and gullies and races, but fish do adventure along them—well, bass do for sure—and if you keep an eagle eye on your float, and don't mind having to make a fresh cast every few seconds, and don't mind being caught up many times on underwater obstructions—why, then, this can be a productive and wildly exciting method of fishing. When a fish is hooked in a little cut like this he really panics, he moves like a streak in several directions, and you have to keep contact with him all the way.

When I was using my ten-foot sea trout rod as a float rod, I had to use small and needle-sharp hooks to make sure that I got them struck home—owing to the extreme suppleness of the rod, you understand. I fancy this is a good thing because it got me into the habit of honing up the hook point *regularly*—examining it every single cast, touching it up with the slip of emery every half dozen casts. The sea bed knocks hell out of a hook. I like thin-gauge, fine-wire hooks, but they are susceptible to the bashing they get around rocks. Of course, you don't really need to use small hooks for bass, which have big mouths, but you can usually hook even a large-mouthed fish well with a small fine hook, whereas a big meat-hook type takes some pulling in—but not much pulling out.

Yes, the carp rod pre-eminent for float fishing from the rocks. But for spinning, which is really the *crème de la crème*

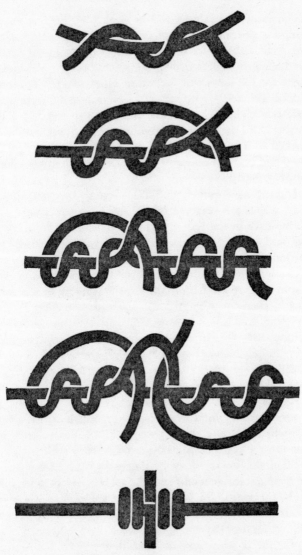

19. Bloodknot for joining lengths of line.

99

of the game, the salmon rod is ideal. I've now given up using my dear old split cane salmon spinning rod—not before time, either—having acquired this very king of rods, the hollow fibreglass Milbro Mariner. It is a royal instrument for the work (as for many other jobs). You may indeed get away with using a seven-foot light spinning rod, but eight foot is a lot nicer, not so much for the casting as for the playing and landing of the fish when you've hooked it. The Mariner, like the salmon rod, is 9 ft. 6 in. long, and casts an ounce or an ounce and a half very comfortably. But suit yourself, of course.

I mentioned earlier that those crank-handled casting rods, which are very pretty and feel somehow 'right' and businesslike in the hand, were usually short, about five to five and a half feet, and designed to take the closed-face version of the fixed-spoon reel. True enough; but there *is* a much longer, double-handed version, such as the Abu Caster 151 at seven feet, the Abu Diplomat at the same length, even the Abu Atlantic 460 with the offset locking reel seat, which is 9 ft. long. All these are double-handed casting rods which will accept a light multiplying reel very happily. They have a rather different 'feel' from the traditional spinning rod, but who cares so long as it's a nice feel? And they do the job, superbly well.

Rarely indeed, when rock fishing, will you see the quarry right on the surface (as you often see them out at sea, when they are chasing the shoals of sprats and brit). No, the reason they are nosing round the rocks at all is because the lower slopes of the rocks, well under water, harbour agreeable food-forms in their crevices and their abundant weed. So you should be spinning fairly deep —but *how* deep, or rather how deep you dare go before fouling up on the rocks and weed and bottom stones, why, that is what you have to discover for yourself by patient experiment, trial and error. Error can be expensive:

it's no good pretending, spinning from the rocks can on occasion be expensive in terms of lost, snagged tackle. And spinning lures cost a mint of money these days. This is why I recommend that when you have fixed up your spinning gear, before you actually start spinning as such, you make a few trial casts with something both inexpensive and attractive on the end of the line. And what could fill the bill better than a sprat on a spinning flight?

True, even a spinning flight, which is little more than a pin to go through the dead fish, a couple of vanes to make it revolve, a swivel and a pair of hooks, even this costs money. But any modestly handy man can make himself

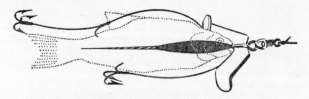

20. Spinning flight for dead fish, such as sprats.

up a score of spinning flights instead of watching television, or even while watching television. All you need is a pair of tin snips to shape the vanes (or your wife's kitchen scissors), a pair of pliers with a wire cutting device built into them, a hank of trace wire, a swivel, a couple of hooks, and a nail to form the spike which is thrust into the dead bait fish's body. (You cut the head off the nail with a hacksaw, and hammer one end flat for an inch to take the vanes, and, via a $\frac{1}{16}$ in. hole, the swivel.)

Nothing could be simpler, and after you have made a few of these and caught the odd fish on them, you get so cocky your friends won't come near you. I've known a chap decide to use bleak instead of sprats, when there were no sprats available at his fishmonger, miles inland. Catching the bleak took him ten minutes flat, from his association water on a very dull bit of river. He didn't actually catch any sea fish on his bleak spinner, though. He was so steamed-up at having no sprats and having to lose time catching his bleak, he drove to the coast with his foot half-way through the floorboards. His little old heap wasn't really up to it and a half-shaft went just when he'd reached the really lonely bit over the mountains. It did seem a pity. Still, I've no doubt bleak would have done all right.

True, they are soft little fish which break up quickly, but so for that matter are sprats. All the best books, in the old days, used to tell you how to bind your spinning fish

21. Artificial spinner—the long narrow spoon.

on to the spinning flight with cotton. When you've accomplished this neatly while huddling on a slippery rock ledge with cold spray dashing over you and your fingers either blue with cold or streaky-red with abrasions, you can apply for life membership of the Holier Than Thou Chum Club.

Never mind. A sprat on a spinning flight is a good proposition, and well worth persevering with. Especially for these first dozen or so casts while you are prospecting, finding where the fish are, how deep, what the walls and bottom are like. If you catch a fish or two while you're experimenting, you'll feel rather chuffed, as they say in the Brigade of Guards (other ranks section). But when it comes to chancing your real shop-bought spinners, you will be confused by the ecstatic variety on show and sale.

Who can help you here? I personally am very fond of fluttering little bar-spoons, and undoubtedly the fish find them very intriguing, but they are very light, really too light for this job, and although mackerel go mad about them more often than not, it means that you have to use a weight on the trace to get casting distance and to sink them far enough. This is really undesirable: you are fishing fairly badly restricted spaces, as a rule, it is accuracy you want more than distance, and the weight should therefore all be concentrated at the tip, the very end—it's like throwing a dart or shooting an arrow.

But if you do have to attach lead, so be it. You should have a trace about two or three feet long, no longer,

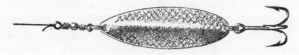

22. Typical conventional spoon.

attached to your reel line via the inevitable swivel. You can hook a quickly detachable Hillman Lead on to the *top* eye of the swivel, thereby lessening any tendency to line kink; or you can incorporate a costly though very lovely Wye lead in the trace—it carries its own swivel; or you can wrap the line round the incisions in a spiral lead; or you can simply fold a half-moon lead over the *top* eye of the swivel. This is the easiest method. A half-moon lead comes to you as a full moon, with a hole in it, like a Polo mint. It is folding it over that makes it a half moon. I like that lead: it is its own built-in anti-kink device.

Of course you can use Devon Minnows, sinking plugs, anything in the armoury: but I guess the most popular and effective spinner is one version or another of the celebrated long narrow spoon. This really does work: especially the sort which is thick and very heavy for its size, and which has a subtle kink or twist built into it which gives it a lovely capricious flutter and flash and wobble. This type of spoon—it comes in many variations —is not only attractive to bass and pollack, but has the weight you need to flick it out.

Don't be put off if the tide rips mighty fast and swirly past your rocks. Bass won't be put off: they are great-hearted adventuring fish, the only fish, really, that will come right inshore and nose among the rocks in such a swirl of heavy water. Fish the race with confidence—and plenty of weight on your spoon.

Spinning is emphatically *not* a matter of simply chucking your lure out and stolidly winding it back in. By no means. You can work a touch of artistry into your retrieve—indeed, you'll have to. Let the bait rise and fall in the water, varying its depth partly by the speed of your retrieve (the faster you wind the more it will climb in the water) and partly by raising and lowering the rod tip. Vary the path of the lure, too, laterally, by wagging the rod, even swinging it from side to side. Vary the speed of the retrieve at all times—slow down, twitch it, give a quick couple of turns, stop dead (for a second only!) start again slow, accelerate, decelerate—do everything you can to give your lure an erratic course, down there in the water. Let the rod and line and lure be an extension of your arms and hands: think lure: think fish: project your senses like antennae (which they are) down into the water with that wriggling, quivering, sinuous, dodging, presumably injured, pitiful little lure.

You may also fish a prawn, live or dead, or two prawns for that matter, if you have them, from your rock position. Bass like them very much and will show their appreciation. I don't think the old sliver of mackerel bait really comes

23. Light spoon.   24. 'Jigger' lure.

into its own here, excellent though it is elsewhere. Worms may be used, but I think prawn and shrimp and shellfish baits would be more natural and therefore perhaps better.

In the North where men are men they catch coalfish from the rocks; even from cliff tops. Down farther south bass and mackerel are the principal quarry, though pollack are a significant factor, too. Daytime fishing doesn't produce much in the way of pollack round the rocks, except small ones: dusk and dawn patrols *do* produce good specimens.

But even if you are simply jigging up and down with a string of 'feathers' for summer mackerel, or a jigger, you will enjoy a session 'on the rocks'.

I should say that I have mentioned only the best and

H

most popular fish. When fishing the rocks, especially the gullies and channels between rocks, you may meet almost anything—well, not quite anything, but certainly such fish as ballan wrasse (not very nice), or pout (not much nicer) and there is always a possibility, to put it no higher, of hooking bream, which are delicious.

A long-handled landing net—the same one you use inland—can be quite a help in these rocky situations. True, you may lose it, or trip over it. I've always understood that these things are sent to try us.

Chapter VII

FISHING FROM THE SHORE

From the shore or beach, that is. I've heard it referred to, time and again, simply as 'beach casting'. As if there were nothing more to it than the act of casting. Well, there is a bit more, a good bit more; yet it remains ever and always true that the act of casting really is extremely important —or *can* be, in certain circumstances. Which is why it pays to practise until you can cast your bait out a fair distance. True, you may catch fish ten yards out—by heaven, ten *feet* is enough at times, when the bass come rarin' right in almost to dry land, chasing their prey. But on other occasions, and in other places, you may find that if you cannot get your bait out 100 yards you might as well stay at home.

Sea fish are almost certain to be 'on the feed'—unlike freshwater fish, which don't feed perpetually. So catching them boils down to four simple operations. We may break it down—we *should* break it down—into these four components: (a) Find the fish. (b) Present to its notice a bait which it will accept. (c) Hook it. (d) Land it.

So simple. But you can go wrong on all four counts.

(a) This must be ranked as the first and most important need, for without it, all is lost. Now where, when faced by a ghastly great expanse of ocean, do you decide that the fish are? They aren't just anywhere and everywhere, be sure of that. They are, in a crisp word, where the food is. In a succinct phrase, they are in the larder, rummaging on the shelves. Now where is the fish's larder?

The answer is as various as the types of shore or beach

which you may fish. Fortunately, it is entirely logical.

If you are fishing a plain sandy shore with a gentle slope, the fish will be coming in behind the breakers, probably behind the third breaker, though I wouldn't like to bet on it. Maybe the fourth. The waves are hammering the sand and innumerable worms and tiny organisms are being washed out by the surf, and the fish are following up. So on this sort of shore—cast well out into the breakers and you won't be wasting your time entirely.

However, you can improve on that general rule very considerably if you will take the trouble, or spare the time, to examine the area at dead low water. You really should do a Sherlock Holmes bit on this—it may prove the most important, the most productive part of your expedition. Note carefully, first, if there are any outcrops of rocks —trifling little bits of things they may be, but they matter. Merely a patch of stubborn stones rising a tiny distance proud of the sand will do. Fish head straight for these irregularities. Well, it stands to reason, doesn't it? Faced with a great vast featureless stretch of underwater sand, wouldn't you, if you were a fish, head for anything that looked slightly interesting, anything to make a change? And, of course, there is food for fish lurking around those bits of rock.

Another feature which the eagle eye should spot, and note, is any depression, any rivulet, any gully or channel whatsoever. This is really important. Fix it in your mind: take bearings and hang on to them. The sea is going to look awfully featureless when the tide comes in. Line up any landmarks that are going to enable you to pinpoint the deepest gully or creek you can find (or, of course, patch of rock) when it is hidden under the eau. It is very near a stone-cold certainty that fish coming in behind the advancing surf are going to spend a lot of time in nosing around those gulleys, pills, creeks, rivulets or rocks. For they are where the small stuff lives and hides, they provide some shelter and much sustenance. If, when the tide comes in, you can place your bait spot-on, bang where you planned to do, right on the spot where the fish are hunting around, you're home and dry. Well, not dry exactly.

But of course not all beaches are gently shelving sand. There is the steep-to shingle beach, any amount of it. This is a very different proposition. Shingle, as is well known, is sterile from the point of view of fish food. The stones composing it take a fearful hammering from the sea, nothing can live in them. So it's not a lot of use letting your bait lie on the pebbles.

Nor, though, is it a lot of use hurling your bait out on to the sandy bottom which lies beyond the shingle. For the fish ain't all that likely to be swanning around on it. Where *are* they, then? They are crowding into the bait parlour or snack supermarket which is strictly localised at that very point where the shingle gives way to the sand. There and virtually nowhere else are they to be found. And for why? I'll tell you why, comrade and brother-in-arms. They are huddling and elbowing there, in the ditchy little bit of a gully at the junction of sand and shingle, because it is precisely here, at the angle between the shingle bank and the sandy gentle bottom, that food galore is put at their disposal. What happens is that the waves wash and knock the abundant small food life out of the sand—and hurl it landwards until it is abruptly stopped, halted and anchored by this slope of shingle which rises from the relatively level sand bed. So a fair mass of food accumulates just at that point, I should perhaps say that *line* where sand and shingle meet. Fish have had longer to find this out than you have: they've been doing it for countless generations. So they'll be there, nosing around. And your bait had better be there, too.

Just how far out the shingle changes over to the sandy bottom, needless to say, is a fact which you simply have to know. Kind local anglers may confide in you. Unkind local anglers may conceivably try to mislead you. You may copy their casts, though of course you may be wasting time by doing so—they may not be locals at all, they may be strangers as clueless as you. No, the one certain way of finding out is to have a real good gander at dead low water. Generally speaking the junction is possible to spot—it may be the low-water mark itself, though not necessarily. But you can always consult an Admiralty chart, ask at the Town Hall, or even take a swim.

Find it you must. On such a beach, it will make all the difference to your sport to know where it is. True, you always stand quite a fair chance of catching the odd fish on the sandy reaches well beyond the junction of sand and shingle. But fewer, and fewer by far, than if you can hit on the line itself.

The right spot isn't always 'a mile' out, as at Dungeness with its famous, or infamous, 'Dustbin'. It may be close in: all depends on the steepness of the beach, the underwater geography which is so important, and so interesting, to learn.

Too often it *is* a devil of a distance. Keep plugging away until you have that 100-yard cast under your belt. In judo terms, your Black Belt.

And now let me say right away, just to cheer you up, that I have caught bass when wading in up to my knees —caught them *behind* me. Yes, I mean that bass have been between me and dry land—when I've been only a matter of a dozen yards out in the water. This has happened when wading in thigh boots, spinning parallel with the shore, off the Sussex coast—why, God bless us all, I was within casting distance, at the time, of a row of bungalows. Their owners could have caught bass that day from their bedroom windows. This was not far from Wittering, I may say, thereby starting a stampede. (But where you'll park your car is another story.) Oh yes, the day does dawn when bass come right in almost to dry land, dashing in after their prey, wildly excited in the spume and surf. Though the day I'm remembering was actually calm . . .

Beaches vary in another way—the way they face. The Atlantic storm beach is an extreme example. Facing the might and power of the open sea, it is lashed and pounded by gales which started, perhaps, a thousand miles out in the ocean. Such beaches, fully exposed to the West, taken an almighty hammering during gales. Needless to say it is no use fishing them at the height of the storm. Even the bold bass won't face that crippling surf. And even if the bass could, you would never be able to keep your bait down, not even with a stone of lead. The power of the surf and the undertow to move great weights has to be seen to be believed. It can be seen by any interested onlooker in oilskins who cares to anchor himself somewhere and watch the rocks a-roll.

The time to fish a storm beach is when the storm is over. Not the moment it goes quiet, but during the next three days, after a real good 'un. Preferably, I would say, about four tides after the peak or crest of the storm. Then you will find great lakes of spume and foam lying between waves which are still powerful, though calming down. The bass will be there then, avid for the multitudinous food supply that has been washed up out of the sand and grit.

Not all bits of beach, of course, even in the exposed parts of the coast, actually face right into the eyes of the wind. The coast is often very ragged—bays and promontories giving you a choice of three different aspects all within a brief stroll. Use them accordingly. Fish the bit where the sea is just nasty enough.

Don't omit to make full use of such heaven-sent aids to fish and fishing as that curious invention of man, the groyne. Wherever groynes have been built out to sea in an effort to resist erosion, use them—use them at all times, but especially after rough weather, or even during rough weather. It will not have escaped your agile mind that the sheltered side of a groyne does not only provide low-water shelter for sunbathers and picnickers: it provides high-water shelter for fish, from the hammer and pressure of the tide. When a heavy sea is running, there are havens of relative peace to be found right up close in on the sheltered side of a groyne. Note which way the sea is running—it often runs not straight in, but at a sharpish angle to the land —and use the groyne accordingly. You can often fish right up against the woodwork (or stonework) with great success. But this is real heavy-weather advice.

Some anglers stand on top of the groynes, thereby obtaining a pleasing illusion of effortless superiority. I doubt if it is really worthwhile, apart from the not inconsiderable danger of being washed away in the furious undertow should you lose your footing. You don't need the extra casting distance if the fish are coming in literally under your feet, and I've never thought it too good an idea to stand over the fish. It isn't quite so important, to practise the time-honoured fresh water doctrine of 'fine and far-off'; but sea fish aren't all idiots, it's still better to 'study to be quiet', absurd though such advice may seem when you can't hear yourself shout for the noise of the wind and the waves. But a habit of dissimulation, of caution and stealth, is a good thing to acquire. In fishing, I mean: not in the human dealings of life, where a frank and manly straightforwardness is much to be preferred. Though I don't know . . .

(b) Baits for shore fishing are as various as for anywhere else. Some say this, some say that. Ask around locally, as

25. Baiting-up with squid.

always, and use whatever is to hand. You can usually buy a grisly species of highly emaciated and under-nourished lugworm. Well, it works, if you can force yourself to load the hook with what amounts to folding money. If you can't gather your own bait, you just don't have any option but to pay. Never forget, though, that the blithe locals who are selling you this rubbish have not actually parted with money for it themselves. Ho no, monsewer: they have taken a gentle stroll at low water and done a bit of back-bending. Which is what you should aim to do, unless, like me, you have a rooted and almost religious objection to back-bending.

Well, there it is: you pays your money *or* you takes your choice. When an abler and younger man, prone to drink excessive quantities of stout and eat lots of unhealthy fried food, I spent hundreds of hours bent double, digging away with a garden fork for ragworms and lugworms, up-ending razor fish, scrambling over rocks and dabbling in rock pools and prizing off all manner of shellfish thereto adhering, barging about with shrimping nets, even setting curious and highly ingenious baited traps for prawns. It's all good clean healthy fun, and saves you pounds. Do try it. The snag is that you get so keen on bait collecting you don't have any time (or energy, for that matter) left for actually fishing with it.

It is my firm opinion, and I don't have many like that, that you can catch fish from the shore on virtually any fishy bait.

But I keep on meaning to experiment with butcher's offal—the sort of grisly stuff from a cow's or sheep's insides that honest women sold themselves to unscrupulous butchers to get a pound of, during the war. (Or so I've heard tell.) I've not had the nerve to do it yet, but may I say on a slightly more serious note that I really don't see why not—a hungry fish, and thank heavens most of them are in a perpetual tizzy of hunger, or at least appetite, or greed, which tots up to the same thing, will eat almost anything nutritious in the high-protein line. Bass are known to fancy a bit of something high—high tea for a good bass may be a hunk of herring long past its prime, a fish head that the cat wouldn't look at, a deplorable remnant of mackerel that failed to find a friend ashore. So why shouldn't they fancy a morsel of lights or tripe?

Among the baits *known for certain* to have procured fish for the shore fisherman are lugworm, ragworm, squid, bits of squid, cuttlefish, razorfish, any shellfish you care to name, pieces of mackerel, sand eel, herring, pilchard, and kipper. Yes, mate, kipper. My own trouble is that I like the kipper too much to share it.

One of the interesting innovations in pike fishing, during the 1950s, was the use of sprats and herrings as bait. These salty sea fish began to be used as pike baits on waters that had never felt a touch of salinity—and very successful they were, and still are. Up till then, it had been assumed that only freshwater fish, dace and roach and gudgeon and the like, were suitable baits for pike. I really don't see why the reverse should not hold good—a roach for a bass, say, a piece of dace for a cod. One day when I'm feeling desperate, certain that I shall fail to procure the usual sea-food baits, I mean to take a few freshwater small fish along, and try it out.

I'd like to return to the question of sole fishing, for a moment. Few anglers fish for them from the beach deliberately, but more might do so if it were commonly realised how many soles come in quite close, and how easy they are to catch *on the right tackle*. I think you should choose a relatively calm day, when you can use your very small hook (size 6 at most, 8 for preference) baited with a small scrap of fish or worm, and, using a very light paternoster or better still a free-running leger on fine nylon, not more than five or six pounds breaking strain, fish of set purpose for those delicious fish. They don't run large and they don't, of course, really rank as a sport-fish: but who cares when they come to table? I like to try this method with a glass carp or Avon rod, a one-ounce lead, a fixed-spool reel and a bit of real creamy calm surf, hardly recognisable as surf. Fish near the low water mark —they rarely follow the rising tide inshore.

(c) Hooking the fish is sometimes a very simple operation, but it can be quite baffling, even frustrating. There is considerable argument amongst experienced anglers on this very point. Now sole, which we have just been discussing, hook themselves. Some cod will hook themselves, sometimes: others won't. Bass are immensely variable in their bites. It is notorious that the smaller ones *do* go at the bait so madly that they often hook themselves. But big bass can bite so gently that you hardly feel them. The question that arises is, How do I strike? Or do I strike at all?

Generally speaking it is a safe plan to strike when you feel a pluck, strike decisively and with malice aforethought. You may miss a few fish this way, but fewer, I think, than you will miss if you leave it to them. Some fish give a 'rattling' bite—a real chain of little knocks in tremendously quick succession, described by tradition as a rattle and recognisable as such. Bream are such biters and so, conspicuously, are plaice. The take of a codling is decisive, but the approach of a real big cod is more deliberate. One of the factors is that to attract a real big cod, you must use a real big bait—a whole bunch of worms, for example, if it's worms you are using.

When cod fishing, I think you may safely leave it to nature. You may certainly use a rod rest, which takes the strain off vastly. Elaborate tripods are on sale, fit to carry expensive cameras. There are bipods, which are utterly adequate, the fishing rod forming the third side of the triangle. Or you can lash a pair or trio of sticks or canes together and cope perfectly. You really do want a rod rest when fishing for hours, possibly all night, for cod—it may be hard weather, for cod, though available in the smaller sizes at almost all seasons, come to their glory in autumn and winter. Then you may well want to light a fire, or at least a portable gas stove, and brew up, or fry bangers or bacon, or both. You really must keep up not only your strength but your spirits. A tired, hungry fisherman is an indifferent fisherman, in the most exquisitely exact sense of the word.

Not that it needs a really alert angler to spot a good big cod bite. Bang goes the rod tip. You will find you have all the time it takes to seize the rod, strike hard with an enthusiastic backward swing, and reel in. With the heavy

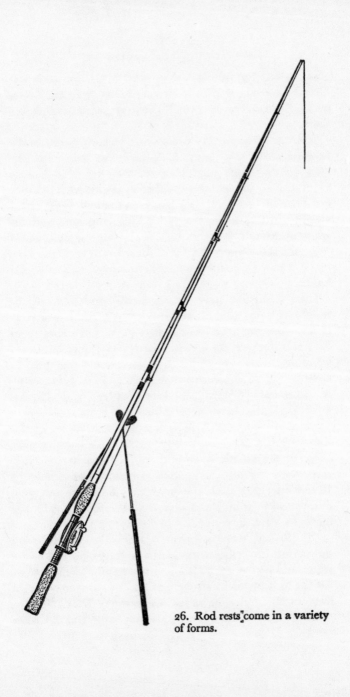

26. Rod rests come in a variety of forms.

gear needed for fishing out in winter surf for cod, you should have no problem in driving home those big strong hooks. Even so, one day, you'll live to regret not sharpening them.

Bass are a more tricky proposition when it comes to the hooking. As I said, some bass, including big ones, bite very gently. Some on taking the bait in their mouths swim strongly towards the shore, don't ask me why, but they do. Thereby taking off your line even the light stress of the weight, putting a big floppy bag into the line, and the wind up you. I know it isn't universally agreed, but I think the safe thing when bass fishing in the surf is to keep the rod in your hands and strike smartly at the slightest knock.

Even when you have got the hook home and felt the weight of your bass, all is not over—not until you have him on dry land, and not always then. On feeling your fish, belt back up the beach smartly. You may be fishing standing actually in the water; you should certainly be right at the water's edge if not actually in it. Now get up on indisputably dry land, and keep the pressure on. There is some similarity between playing a bass and playing a salmon, or a sea trout. You have to keep a strain on, in case the hook has only just lightly snicked it on the outside, even, of the mouth—this is more likely to happen with those very big ones, that take so gently and cunningly. If the line goes slack the hook may fall out, and your chagrin will go on increasing as your estimate of its size increases. As it surely will.

(d) But the worst moment is when the bass feels the shingle on his belly, when his back comes up out of the water and he realises he is about to enter the alien element. Added to his panicky struggle at that moment may be the force of the undertow as the wave surges back. Needless to say you use a wave to help the fish home and dry—but unless you pounce on him smartly he may yet get back into the water. A hand in that spiny, wounding gill cover is the only sure answer.

'Everyone' recommends the use of at least two hooks, often three. It seems to be the universal method, so naturally I pass it on to you, as in duty bound. I am in a minority, possibly a minority of one, in that I vastly prefer to use only one hook and one bait. Doubtless it reduces my chances of hooking a fish, but doubtless it improves my morale by the certain knowledge it brings that I am using the most simplified gear possible, in the most sporting way. On a steep-to beach I use a rolling leger, which sways and wanders around nicely.

I use a simple rolling leger for cod, too: simplicity and pared-to-the-bone terminal tackle appeals to me deeply, though I am as big a sucker for elaborate casting gear, rods and reels, as any man.

While beach fishing for cod you may well catch whiting, for which you need no particular prescription, or dabs, which are very tasty indeed, despite their small size and lack of fighting quality. Well, how should they fight, when hooked on massive gear designed to haul in cod weighing many times their weight? But no-one objects to a dab on the plate, I find. If you really want to go dab fishing, just dab fishing, there is no law against it whatsoever. Rig up a lighter rod, of course, with the sort of gear you use for sole—but a bigger hook will serve, say a No. 6 or even No. 4. Bait it with lugworms for preference.

Worms will also attract whiting, if you should wish to concentrate on those fish, which are rather smaller in the south than in the north and which are much nicer than they smell when casually boiled for the cats. Sprats or herring pieces, always available in winter, seem the best bait. Again, though, you are more likely to hook whiting when not really trying. More a boat fisher's fish.

Perhaps a distinction should be made between the codling and the cod. The cod grows to a great size, twenty-pounders are common; the codling is simply a young cod of about four or five pounds. Codling is to cod as lamb is to mutton. Of course they are exactly the same fish at different stages of growth, but their habits vary a bit. Thus the small stuff seems to hang around, whereas the big chaps come in close only during the autumn and winter. In really bitter weather cod come amazingly close inshore. Whereas very cold water drives most fish offshore to the warmer deeps, where they go to spawn, anyway.

Chapter VIII

ESTUARY FISHING

The freshwater fisher converted to estuary fishing immediately feels at home—and also feels a great surge of new optimism and pleasure. For though truly sea fishing, or at least salt-water fishing, estuary fishing has some features in common with the most exciting styles of river fishing. Compared with other methods it is relatively confined —you have *banks* to play with—but is still very much the salt, the dear old tidal ozoney margin between land and sea, and therefore exhilarating; and the fish available are greatly more worthwhile than any the river fisher ever meets, save of course the princely game fish.

Of course you meet those too. Never forget that sea trout are caught in estuaries, marvellous fresh-run sea trout like bars of solid silver, straight in from the sea and absolutely at their prime. You take them by spinning or by fishing a tandem or demon lure with a fly rod and a synthetic (*not* silk) fly line. Not all rivers have a run of sea trout, of course, but those that do . . .

There are many occasions on the estuaries of really sporting rivers when one finds both bass and sea trout running at the same time. On those thrice-blessed western estuaries you can catch both, with worms, drift-lining, or with the spinner high in the water, or with the fly. I am thinking of fishing from a boat, actually. Estuarial fishing offers fun both to the boat fisherman and the man who stays ashore. But many times, with my feet firmly on the ground, I have spun for both species. This is a just an appetiser, an example of how royally rewarding a good estuary to a good clean river can be.

I know that to a great many converts, estuary fishing will have the greatest appeal, partly because it demands techniques with which they are familiar from their riverside experience, partly because it is the very cream of light tackle fishing in salt water. It is quite true that if you want to try salt water fishing without going to any fresh expense, your freshwater tackle is likely to serve. Well, of course, if you come straight from match fishing, if you have been a toothpick-float specialist accustomed to whipping out thousands of immature bleak and roach in order to win some sweep or trophy, then you will not be ideally equipped—in tackle or in mental equipment either. No, a stiff, frail, quick-tipped match fishing rod is *not* quite the

27. Tandem fly—Demon or Terror lure.

thing. But the Avon-style coarse fishing rod has its place, the pike and carp rods come strongly into their own (or the salmon rod, of course) and although you may still use genuine sea tackle such as you need in other modes of sea fishing, you can get by without it. All of which is a help to the beginner.

The Avon-style rod of ten or eleven feet in length is in fact a perfect weapon for mullet fishing, and a light 'trout' spinning rod is perfectly OK for spinning for bass (and sea trout). I have ruined one Avon rod fishing for flounders, and recommend, on the whole, that the carp rod is the ideal weapon. It has just that bit more to it in terms of strength—and remember it isn't the fish which is going to kill the rod, it is the snags you may have to haul out, the general wear and tear of casting slightly more weight than you usually need in thinner fresh water, and odd weed snags and rock snags and of course the quite severe attacks which salt air makes on any gear. Whatever you choose, it should ideally be a fairly long and fairly light rod, if you are to get the cream of the sport.

Estuaries vary enormously, as do the rivers of which they are the final segment. It's not much use fishing the estuary of a heavily polluted river, naturally. Clean estuaries vary from little creeks to vast areas, almost lagoons, which empty and fill twice a day as the tide changes. Whatever the geography of the estuary, it is important that you know it; and the more intimately, the better. Local knowledge is a great help, of course, but it may be even more helpful to scrutinise the area yourself, at dead low tide. Just looking at an estuary at high water isn't going to tell you very much. And the fact is that estuaries are not uniformly productive of fish over their whole area: there are taking spots and relatively barren spots, and the only way you can tell the one from the other (unless of course you find a kindly and obliging local character who will educate you) is to examine the lie of the land at low tide.

You will see that the bed of the estuary is scored by rivulets, gulleys, pills and what you might almost call ditches—apart from the main channel of the river. It is quite important to know these depressions, for when the sea fish come into the estuary on the making tide, avid to feed on the rich marine life of worms and shellfish that the estuary protects and nourishes, they certainly don't want to waste any time. They come trickling up the deeper channels as soon as the tide begins to fill. And, moreover, it is these deeper bits, which sometimes never dry out, that harbour most food. So try to examine the lie of the land before you start to fish: learn where the deep river channel runs, and where these subsidiary runners run. The first fish to arrive, and the last to leave, will be travelling in them. True, when the water is high it isn't so important to know the latent depths, but you want to get as much fishing out of every tide as possible.

It is generally bass and mullet (and, where present, sea trout) that run in from the sea. The bass and mullet stay only a short while and depart as the tide departs: the sea trout usually run on up towards the headwaters, for they have entered the river of their birth in order to spawn. However, even sea trout sometimes take a few tides to make up their minds, hanging around the mouth of the river as if uncertain, and reluctant to commit themselves.

The species which inhabit the estuary permanently, and do not run in and out with the tide, are flounders. I don't say they never go to sea, but certainly they are to be found in the estuary all the year round, sometimes well up the river in brackish water which may also sustain some brown trout (if it is that sort of river) which are often called slob trout.

Flounder fishing in an estuary is not perhaps so exciting as bass fishing, well it certainly isn't, but the bass aren't always to be had and the flounders are. Flounders even more than other fish of the estuary seem to stick to clearly defined channels. It is as if flounders have runs like rat runs or fox runs. Whereas you may meet roving bass almost anywhere, once the water is high.

It is rather mournful work to catch estuarial flounders on heavy tackle, but with an Avon or carp rod, a fixed-spool reel loaded with five or six pound line, a small lead of about an ounce or even less, and a lugworm or ragworm for bait, you will surely hook some using the simple running leger rig. A plump flounder fried with bacon and mushrooms is a dish for an epicure or a very honest man. The flesh is a little darker and richer in flavour that that of the white-fleshed flat fish such as dabs and plaice, and maybe it is an acquired taste, like the Guinness that goes so well with it.

A fairly popular and very effective method of fishing for flounders is to drag a baited spoon along the bottom. The spoon is a pretty big affair, and the hook trace trails from it, anything from three to six inches away. The hook is baited with worm as usual—it is the bait which the fish grabs, not the spoon. In fact the spoon is merely a method of attracting the flounder to the bait. It flips and flops slowly along the sea bed, stirring up the sand. Some anglers

28. Flounder spoon.

simply use a fair-sized lead, stopped by a swivel six inches above the baited hook, to do the same job of creating a minute disturbance which, it is hoped, will attract the attention of a nearby fish who might otherwise not notice. It works, too.

Bass, too, are often caught with this form of bottom fishing, and certainly ragworm legered is attractive to them when they are down in the water. Personally I have never done so well with lugworm, though this is the angler's stand-by in some districts. But bass may also be caught higher in the water, and you have to experiment a bit to find out at what height they are coming in *today*. It isn't necessarily the same approach two tides running. This is where the float fisherman scores, of course—he can control the depth at which his bait rides in the water.

One snag of bottom fishing in an estuary is the presence of innumerable small greenish crabs. These are bait robbers *par excellence*. A way out is to use that trick of slitting a cork half way through and slipping it on the hook link a couple of inches above the hook. Of course, if you happen to be fishing from a boat, at anchor, it is easy to use a pater-noster with the hook link well above the reach of crabs. This works well if you *can* use a boat or a jetty from which you can lower your tackle down almost vertically. But in strong currents, or fishing from the bank, it isn't so easy, and then I recommend the leger with the cork.

Whether you use a boat, or fish from the bank, will depend on factors which I cannot anticipate. Some big estuaries are so wide that a boat is pretty well essential to give you proper coverage of the good spots—especially that good spot just inshore of the sand bar which partially seals the mouth of so many estuaries. Estuarial boat fishing is very fine: you can, for example, indulge in drift-lining, sending a live sand eel or prawn or just a worm working down the current. This is marvellous fun, on occasion. You control the depth at which your bait is working by varying the amount of lead on the swivel. Naturally you can send a float down the tide just as easily. They are excellent ways—especially the drift-lining —of exploring the middle depths until you hit on the depth at which today's fish are taking.

But when the bass are showing right on the surface, then the answer surely is spinning. This is the very cream of the sport. You sometimes see the bass tearing along, actually showing on the surface as they hunt the fry with that immense gusto and avidity of the great-hearted predators they are. If ever there was a time to send your silver bar-

29. Baiting with prawn.   30. Heavy eccentric spoon

spoon or long narrow spoon among them, this is it. Spin it *very fast* and riding high in the water. Never mind what I said about spinning low and slow—that was rock fishing, this is estuary fishing, and the bass, when they are in this surface-showing mood, want a silvery little spinner that rides high and goes like the clappers. It is all in tune with the mood of the moment: you will surely feel in your bones, if you have the heart of a fisherman, that this is the appropriate method for the moment.

How small a spinner depends—no-one knows for sure what it depends on, exactly, but it is well known that one day a tiny little one-inch spoon, or Devon minnow, is the answer, another day they want a much larger spoon. Personally I think it is probably a question of the average size of the fry they are chasing. If it is a shoal of tiny immature fingerlings, they have tiny fish on the brain. If it is more mature specimens that are shoaling together, that is the size they are accustomed to and their reaction is automatic.

Please don't think this is fanciful: it is established that some fish do become so habituated to a certain diet, so *pre-occupied*, as my old pal Richard Walker put it, that for the time being they literally won't look at anything else. This is true of some freshwater fish some of the time, and of some estuary fish it is likewise true. I think this may be the answer to the bass's preferences, today for a little 'un, tomorrow for a bigger one. (We often find that one day the only bait the flounder wants is lugworm, another day it's ragworm. If you haven't got the right answer you may be up the creek in the literal sense and the metaphorical one, too.)

I must say that where it is convenient to take a boat out on the estuary, it does give you a certain freedom and thrill which bank fishing cannot counterfeit. This is not only true of the greater variety of techniques which become available to you—you can 'cover' the fish so much better from a boat, you can drift your lure down the current, you can fish the vertical paternoster, you can inch up within range when using the fly rod—but there is a further advantage, on some rivers: you can follow the fish as they move upstream and back down again. Bass, certainly, don't hang about: they are going in on the tide the whole time, and when the tide begins to turn, they are off back to sea even faster. True, if you can move freely along the bank, either on foot or by bike or even by car, you can fish various points within the scope of one tide: but it's far easier to follow the fish afloat, anchoring at a good spot, up-anchoring and moving on a few hundred yards and dropping the hook again. Oh yes, it's a royal progress if you have a nice beamy little boat and a good man at the oars or the engine. On the other hand, when you want to pump ship it isn't always convenient . . .

Never stand up in a dinghy.

Never stand up on the bank either, if you can sit down. Stay out of sight just as you would way back on the clear water stream. Give the fish the benefit of the doubt—they have sharp eyes, alert senses, including a highly developed sense of doubt and fear.

I won't go on about fly fishing for bass, because although it is delightful and I've greatly enjoyed it, it is not quite so sound and reliable a method of taking them, by and large, as spinning. You meet a shoal of bass one day that really seem to prefer the fly, but most days the spinner will do as well or better. This is no hardship to most people, who fancy that fly fishing is somehow exceedingly esoteric, mysterious and in fact damn near mystical. Which it most certainly isn't. It's easy.

The 'fly' used to attract bass is probably a white feather tied quite roughly to a long-shanked tinned hook. It takes a really determined fly fisher to use one of his expensive sea trout or salmon flies in salt water. My own preference is and always has been the relatively inexpensive two- or three-hooked tandem lure, the kind known as a Demon or Terror. This is two gaudy winged flies connected by a morsel of gut or nylon. It is the best of lures for sea trout, in my experience, and will interest bass sometimes, especially if very bright and light in colour. But they seem to like white best in feathers, as they certainly prefer silver in spinners.

I should think it is very agreeable to cast a 'fly' from the bank, using one of those very nice double-handed glass-fibre salmon fly rods that you can get nowadays, twelve or thirteen feet long. I've never tried it, having done all my estuary fly fishing, for sea trout and bass, with the old ten-foot trout rod aforementioned, my faithful companion through many years. The drill is to cast more or less across the set of the current: it brings the fly skirling and skating across, and the take, when it happens, is a dramatic bang that really sets the adrenalin flowing.

I don't hear very much said about plug fishing for bass, yet it is one of the most beguiling techniques available to the enthusiast who doesn't mind risking his money on the end of his line. The plug, if I may remind you, is a curious device shaped very roughly like a fish, with an upturned vane at the head which makes it dive when you reel it in. While under this tension from the line, it wiggles and wobbles, flutters and dives, comes up again, dives down again, all very sinuous and (sometimes!) lifelike.

Jointed plugs make more of a fuss than solid plugs. Some are made of wood, some of plastic. They are probably meant to simulate injured fish trying desperately to get out of the predator's way—which is why it is a terrible mistake to reel too fast once you have cast your plug. It defeats the whole object of the exercise. You reel very slowly, giving all sorts of help to the performance by your masterly command of the rod tip, which you cause to twitch and switch and sway and nod as you reel in at varying speeds, a turn or two quick, a turn or two slow—but never fast in the sense that a Devon minnow has to be kept moving fast. You feel like Colin Davis conducting the BBC Symphony Orchestra.

I am quite fond of plug fishing from the rocks, and in the estuary I sometimes like to have a go when the bass are not quite on top of the water. A bright silvery plug, for preference. There is an American device (now widely copied elsewhere, I believe) called the popping plug. When you hit the reel handle hard, it actually 'pops' —it makes a dramatic little disturbance on the surface which sometimes attracts fish.

But never forget the value of your sprat spun on a spinning

flight. It is an ancient device which costs the least and still works very well.

The fish of the estuary which has probably caused more bad language than any other is the grey mullet. The grey mullet has turned many an honest man to thoughts of crime. It shows itself right on the surface, at times, dawdling along with the dorsal fin clean out the water. You'd think you couldn't miss. But you can. The fact is that many mullet do get caught. I've caught a few gross myself, but while they are travelling on the surface in this temerarious manner, apparently cocking a snook at the angler, they are terribly difficult to catch. So much so that a legend sprang up that they were uncatchable, which is not so. But I think it is true that you only catch them when you find them in the place where they settle down to feed, not when they are showing so boldy, so insouciantly, and on the move.

Mullet fishing is really the very closest thing in sea fishing to the art of the freshwater specialist. You can use light tackle, the Avon rod and a five-pound line and fixed-spool reel are certainly ample; and you can even use freshwater baits. Mullet will take small ragworm, or pieces of ragworm: of that there is not a trace of doubt. But they will also, on occasion, take the cereals which are the standby of the roach and bream and chub fisher—bread, bread-paste plain or with various flavours, bread crust: one hears, too, of macaroni, banana and cheese all being used successfully. And I may say I believe all I hear. There is no point in being dogmatic about what mullet will or will not eat.

Thus I was fishing one calm afternoon on the little estuary of the River Axe, well below Axmouth, in fact at the seaside town of Seaton. There is a deep pool just immediately on the seaward side of the road bridge. I was down on the sand at the water's edge, fishing tiny

ragworms and pieces of ragworm. Various worthy charac-
ters were fishing from the parapet of the bridge itself,
indifferent to the imminent prospect of having their behinds
deeply scored by the wings of passing cars. Just a shade
seaward of me, a most resourceful character was lying
flat on his stomach on the roof of a little pillbox sort of
building, doubtless a shelter for the local fishermen's gear.

Our methods made an entertaining contrast in styles
and in philosophies. The worthies on the bridge were
dangling floats into the water: their lines bore a more than
passing resemblance to ship's hawsers, their rods were
equal to the task, should they be called upon to undertake
it, of hauling the deadweight of a doughty mullet vertically
out of the water and up to the parapet. Their baits seemed
to be an interesting collection of old offal, fish pieces,
lugworm, earthworm, paste, and last week's bacon rind.
The character lying flat on top of the shack, peering out
craftily over the water with only his head showing,
used a stout rod and line too, but no terminal tackle
whatever, save just the hook, tied directly to his line.
And his hook was baited simply with a quite hefty piece of
breadcrust. He simply dapped it on the surface and
minute bits of it broke off gently into the water. He assured
me that he had the bleedin' mullet weighed up, caught
no end of the perishers. I'm sure he was telling the truth.
In fact I know he was.

But this was not his day. Actually none of us did the
slightest good until the top of the tide, that magical moment
when all seems in suspension; high water, when for a
tremulous few minutes there is no flow at all, you seem poised
in a timeless moment snatched from eternity. It was
during this slack-water period that I, using the simplest
light leger and a small hook (I think it was a carp hook, size
6) baited with fragments of ragworm laboriously acquired,
began to get bite after bite. My mullet were not large,

indeed they were far from distinguished; but they were the only mullet being caught, the only fish of any kind being landed that afternoon, and they came ashore with gratifying frequency. Gratifying to *me*, I mean. I did not notice any particular signs of gratification, any outburst of merriment, any especial symptoms of euphoria, among my unfortunate companions. Especially the bums on the bridge.

I claim no credit. It was simply luck. I happened to have the right bait in the right spot. And this is the secret of success at any time. Carry several of these simple lures to ensure that you have the right bait; study the lie of the land and try to put it in the right spot. I'm sure that what made the difference that day was that my lure happened to be fishing at the right depth—i.e., bang on the bottom. Which is where the shoal happened to be routing about.

(The prone character who dapped bread on the surface made quite a killing next day.)

That floating crust dodge certainly is successful at times. So is cheesepaste, breadpaste flavoured with custard powder, cubes of crust, roughly-torn fragments of crumb. I wonder if maggots would work? Why not? I'll try them one day.

I keep saying that, and I mean it when I say it. But the simple truth is that I don't fish of set purpose for mullet except once in a blue moon. As the girl said with a haughty toss of her pretty head, there are better fish to fry.

Mullet really are susceptible to ground-baiting.

I haven't yet mentioned eels, but in some estuaries they are mentioned very frequently, and in terms that would surprise them if they could lip-read. Some estuaries have a big seaward run of eels. These are not to be confused with the conger that haunt the deeps, lurking in rock crevices and skulking among the ruined ribs of wrecks. They are akin, of course, but not the same. The eel of the estuary is the chap who swam in from the Sargasso Sea, where they are bred, travelled up-river in his millions as a tiny elver (nothing tastier or more nutritious than a mass of fried elver) and after some years in inland fresh-water, on reaching sexual maturity, if you'll pardon the expression, set off down-river again to cross the sea to his ancestral home, there to have his one single, solitary sexual spree, propagate his species, and perish.

Perish the thought indeed.

This type of eel, now turning silvery in his sea-going coat, is a nuisance to some anglers, who don't like his sinuous ways; though of course any resemblance to a water snake is pure coincidence if not bosh. You often get a fierce rattling bite at bottom baits meant for other fish, such as flounders, and on striking (not that there is much if any need to strike) find a yard of eel twisting your line into a right mess. Admittedly, this can be annoying, but I have to say I am very partial to eel, fried, jellied, or stewed. And smoked eel is mighty tasty, too, with a pint of best bitter or even a cup of second-best tea; you need thickish fish for smoking, and conger are best of all. You don't have to fish specially for eels: if they are there, and your bait is high-protein and preferably fresh, and on the bottom, you'll catch eels some time or other. Don't look a gift eel in the mouth, by the way: they can bite, those chaps. I dare say that for sheer furious brute energy and persistence, the Life Force run mad, an eel is the equal of anything that breathes. It's awesome.

Chapter IX

AFTERTHOUGHTS AND ALL THAT

This little book is only intended to set the beginner on the right track. It doesn't pretend to be anything like comprehensive. Thus, I haven't gone into big-game fishing. Big game fishing *for beginners?* Not really, I think. Yet it is certainly true that if you have a strong stomach, and a pocketful of hard-earned or even unearned dough, you can go big game fishing without a minute of previous experience.

All you have to do is go to a place like Looe where they specialise in it and make a living at it, and press your money into the horny hand of one of the very good professional skippers. It costs about £5 a head (1976) for a party of six to ten, and for this you get a lot: a reliable boat, local know-how, tackle, bait, pinpoint navigation and security. If you happen to like this sort of gregarious outing you could hardly do better. It is much the best way of finding out whether you really like big game fishing, without incurring all the preliminary expense, which can be considerable. And if you don't catch sharks, you may well catch other, more edible, items.

But I think you can leave big game fishing until you have done a bit of smaller game fishing. Please yourself, though.

Nor have I gone into the question of all those splendid big fish you may catch, in certain circumstances. Skate may be caught from the shore, or a boat, on the bottom; so may the rays, so may tope, of course, which is our smallest shark but still a sizeable hunk of fish. These things come later, I fancy.

Nor have I even mentioned a vast variety of fish which you may well hook—you may hook them first time out! These are fish which few people angle for of set purpose. Some of them are very odd indeed. You may find yourself connected to silly little pout or pouting, fierce but unlikeable wrasse, dogfish, smooth hound, gurnards, monkfish, John Dory, the rock-loving ling, the poisonous weever; or even, if you are very lucky, the desirable turbot, brill or megrim. Never mind. I've told you what I know about the most popular fish which are angled for of set purpose, and well worth angling for. You will assuredly catch some of the sorts which you don't want, and if your luck holds you will also catch uncommon but highly desirable fish without even trying, without even knowing they were there.

This is the glory and benediction of the sea. You 'cast your bread upon the waters', and you never *really* know, not for sure, what is out there waiting, what it is that has taken your bait or lure. Until you see it. The infinite ocean is inexhaustible in its capacity for surprising us. It makes a man humble, but self-reliant; willing to be surprised, capable of wonder, but ever adventuring his lure into the unfathomable sea with new optimism, new hope.

I wish you happiness and heavy catches. Farewell.